T0208620

ICME-13 Topical Surveys

Series editor

Gabriele Kaiser, Faculty of Education, University of Hamburg, Hamburg, Germany

More information about this series at http://www.springer.com/series/14352

Marilyn E. Strutchens · Rongjin Huang
Leticia Losano · Despina Potari
João Pedro da Ponte
Márcia Cristina de Costa Trindade Cyrino
Rose Mary Zbiek

The Mathematics Education of Prospective Secondary Teachers Around the World

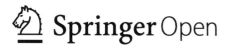

Marilyn E. Strutchens
Department of Curriculum and Teaching
Auburn University
Auburn, AL
USA

Rongjin Huang
Department of Mathematical Sciences
Middle Tennessee State University
Murfreesboro, TN
USA

Leticia Losano
Facultad de Matemática
Universidad Nacional de Córdoba
Córdoba, Córdoba
Argentina

Despina Potari
Mathematics Department Panepistimiouloli
National and Kapodistrian University of Athens
Greece

João Pedro da Ponte
Instituto de Educação
Universidade de Lisboa
Lisbon
Portugal

Márcia Cristina de Costa Trindade Cyrino
Department of Mathematics
State University of Londrina
Londrina
Brazil

Rose Mary Zbiek
College of Education
The Pennsylvania State University
University Park, PA
USA

ISSN 2366-5947   ISSN 2366-5955   (electronic)
ICME-13 Topical Surveys
ISBN 978-3-319-38964-6   ISBN 978-3-319-38965-3   (eBook)
DOI 10.1007/978-3-319-38965-3

Library of Congress Control Number: 2016946302

Printed on acid-free paper

This Springer imprint is published by Springer Nature
The registered company is Springer International Publishing AG Switzerland

Main Topics You Can Find in This "ICME-13 Topical Survey"

- Prospective secondary mathematics teachers' knowledge;
- Prospective secondary mathematics teacher preparation and technology;
- Prospective secondary mathematics teachers' professional identity;
- Prospective secondary mathematics teachers' field experiences.

Contents

Chapter 1
Introduction

The topic study group on the mathematics education of prospective secondary teachers is dedicated to sharing and discussing significant new trends and developments in research and practices related to various aspects of the education of prospective secondary mathematics teachers from an international perspective. As Ponte and Chapman (2016) stated, teacher education is an area in which, although we have developed an understanding about the process of becoming a teacher, many questions still remain open. Our goal in this topic group is to address some of these questions. We discuss major areas in the field, including the nature and structure of teachers' knowledge and its development, models and routes of mathematics teacher education, development of professional identities as prospective mathematics teachers, field experiences and their impact on prospective secondary mathematics teachers' development of the craft of teaching, and use of various technological devices and resources in preparing prospective secondary mathematics teachers. To facilitate the discussion of these issues, the authors of this survey conducted a systematic literature review of studies published in nine international mathematics education research journals[1] during the last decade focused on the following four areas:

Teacher Knowledge. Addressing the nature of prospective mathematics teacher knowledge, theoretical and methodological perspectives, relationship between teacher knowledge, teaching practice, and students' learning as well as the process of prospective teachers' knowledge development in teacher education programs.
Technologies, Tools and Resources. Comparing and synthesizing studies on how prospective mathematics teachers develop knowledge that relates technology, pedagogy and content knowledge.

---

[1]*Educational Studies in Mathematics, International Journal of Science and Mathematics Education, Journal for Research in Mathematics Education, Journal of Mathematical Behavior, Journal of Mathematics Teacher Education, Mathematics Education Research Journal, Mathematical Thinking and Learning, Mathematics Teacher Education and Development, and ZDM Mathematics Education (formerly ZDM—The International Journal on Mathematics Education).*

© The Author(s) 2017
M.E. Strutchens et al., *The Mathematics Education of Prospective Secondary Teachers Around the World*, ICME-13 Topical Surveys, DOI 10.1007/978-3-319-38965-3_1

Teachers' Professional Identities. Synthesizing research findings on the conceptualization of teacher professional identities, the development of teacher identity through pre-service course work and field experiences.

Field Experiences. Synthesizing and discussing research findings on models; mechanisms; roles of prospective teachers, cooperating teachers, and university supervisors; and field experiences.

More details about the methodology adopted for the review are given in the report of each area.

Chapter 2
Current Research on Prospective Secondary Mathematics Teachers' Knowledge

Despina Potari and João Pedro da Ponte

1 Introduction

Teachers' knowledge has been a major focus in the preparation of prospective teachers for a long time. Teachers need to know about the subject that they teach, they need to know how to teach it, and they need to know how to act and behave as teachers. Teacher education institutions organize teacher education programs around three strands, that Winslow and Durand-Guerrier (2007) named as content knowledge, pedagogical knowledge, and didactical knowledge, a distinction based on Shulman's (1986) seminal work that stands as the theoretical basis of a large number of studies in mathematics education. In this chapter, we address research on prospective teacher knowledge in mathematics and didactics of mathematics or knowledge of mathematics teaching.

Ponte and Chapman (2008, 2016) conducted systematic reviews of the research literature from 1998 until 2013 and concluded that some of the important developments in our field are: recognition that mathematical and didactical knowledge required for teaching is of special type; development of ways in teacher education where prospective teachers revisit familiar content in unfamiliar ways to develop the underlying meanings of the mathematics; and understanding the difficulty of prospective teachers to develop knowledge of mathematics teaching and designing tools to promote this knowledge. Although most studies have focused on prospective primary school teachers, there is a recognition that prospective secondary school teachers' (PSMTs)' knowledge of mathematics and mathematics teaching in sec-

D. Potari (✉)
Mathematics Department Panepistimiouloli, National and Kapodistrian
University of Athens, Athens, Greece
e-mail: dpotari@math.uoa.gr

J.P. da Ponte
Instituto de Educação, Universidade de Lisboa, Lisbon, Portugal
e-mail: jpponte@ie.ulisboa.pt

© The Author(s) 2017
M.E. Strutchens et al., *The Mathematics Education of Prospective Secondary Teachers Around the World*, ICME-13 Topical Surveys,
DOI 10.1007/978-3-319-38965-3_2

ondary schools is of a different nature, and new theoretical and methodological frameworks are needed to study it (Speer et al. 2015). In this chapter, we report findings from our survey on studies related to PSMTs' knowledge.

2 Methodology of the Survey

We searched each journal by using the following keywords: "prospective teachers", "future teachers", "teacher candidates", "pre-service teachers", "knowledge", and "secondary". We identified fifty-nine relevant papers, by reading the abstract and the methodology section. In addition, given the importance of large-scale studies on prospective mathematics teachers' knowledge, we identified other relevant papers and reports on these studies. Next, we reviewed and coded the papers and reports according to the following dimensions: (i) focus of the study and its research questions, (ii) main theoretical ideas underpinning it, (iii) methodological elements (setting, participants, instruments/tasks, data and process of data analysis), (iv) main findings, and (v) contribution of the study. Finally, we constructed a table with short descriptions for each paper related to the five dimensions. We first classified the papers in terms of their focus in three main thematic areas, as addressing: (a) the exploration of PSMT knowledge, (b) the impact of teacher education practices on PSMT knowledge, and (c) the process of PMST knowledge development in the context of teacher education programs. Initially, we provide some factual information about the mathematical content areas that the papers address, the dimensions of teacher knowledge, and the theoretical and methodological perspectives used. Then, we discuss the papers grouped in each of the three thematic areas in more detail presenting their main findings and contribution.

3 Basic Information About Research on PSMT Knowledge

3.1 Mathematical Content

Prospective teachers' knowledge of mathematical content has been studied from quantitative and qualitative perspectives. The large-scale TEDS-M international study (Tatto et al. 2012) addressed content knowledge in four content subdomains (number and operations, algebra and functions, geometry and measurement, and data and chance) and in three cognitive dimensions (knowing, applying and reasoning) (Döhrmann et al. 2012; Li 2012). The German study COACTIV (Krauss et al. 2008) is another example of quantitative large-scale study that addresses content knowledge. The papers reviewed, which referred to these studies mostly reported findings regarding content knowledge as a single construct although they

Table 1 The mathematical areas addressed in research studies

Mathematical areas	No. of papers
Specific mathematical content	**22**
Algebra/numbers	10
Geometry	5
Calculus	5
Statistics	2
Mathematical processes	**15**
Problem solving and modeling	11
Reasoning and proof	4
Not specifically defined	**22**

Bold indicates mathematical content (22) includes algebra/ numbers, geometry, calculus and statistics (which values 10+5 +5+2 add up to 22). The same for the mathematical processes (15), that include problem solving and modeling and reasoning and proof (adding also 11+4 = 15)

differentiated between mathematical subjects and between countries as it was difficult to report reliable scores for various mathematical subjects. On the other hand, qualitative studies usually focus on a specific mathematical content or process with emphasis on algebra, problem solving, and modeling, and tend to address this mainly in terms of structure and understanding (Table 1).

3.2 Aspects of PSMT Knowledge

A categorization of the papers according to the aspects of knowledge they address is presented in Table 2. Most studies that focused on PSMT knowledge of mathematics in mathematical contexts used interviews based on mathematical tasks (e.g., Tsamir et al. 2006), mathematical items in survey instruments (e.g., Döhrmann et al. 2012; Huang and Kulm 2012), or interactions in teacher education settings where the solution of a mathematical problem was a main task (e.g., Shriki 2010). Those studies that explored PSMT mathematical knowledge in teaching contexts mostly included settings as the analysis of students' work (e.g., Magiera et al. 2013) or the comparison of different textbooks (e.g., Davis 2009). Shulman's (1986) constructs of content

Table 2 Aspects of PSMT knowledge addressed in research studies

Aspects of PSMT knowledge	No. of papers
Knowledge of mathematics	**41**
Studied in mathematical contexts	27
Studied in teaching context	14
Knowledge of mathematics teaching	**11**
Relationship of knowledge of mathematics and mathematics teaching	**12**

knowledge (CK) and pedagogical content knowledge (PCK) are central to most studies, but some papers draw also on theoretical notions such as the distinction between common content knowledge (CCK) and specialized content knowledge (SCK) of Ball et al. (2008), on the notion of "deep mathematical knowledge" (Hossin et al. 2013) and "teacher knowledge on what else is needed beyond specific content knowledge" (Clark 2012). Despite the fact that many papers strived to address the specific features of PSMT knowledge of mathematics, still a number of them treat PSMTs as students who showed a rather deficient knowledge of mathematics.

Knowledge of mathematics teaching was less central in the research papers reviewed. This refers mostly to teaching of different mathematics topics, and it was often related to mathematics knowledge. The TEDS-M large-scale study (Blömeke et al. 2014) focused on the interrelationships between CK, PCK and general pedagogical knowledge in three participating countries, while the study conducted by Aguirre et al. (2012) included cultural and social elements in teacher knowledge.

3.3 Theoretical and Methodological Perspectives of PSMT Knowledge

The theoretical perspectives adopted by most of the papers belong to the cognitive/constructivist tradition with a few papers using socio-cultural and sociological lenses. The frameworks from Shulman and Ball and her collaborators are major theoretical references while often complemented with other theoretical perspectives. For example, Ticknor (2012) used a situated perspective, "person-in-practice-in-person" of Lerman (2000) to study the mathematical content knowledge developed in an abstract algebra course focusing on how prospective teachers impacted a community of practice, and how practicing in that community impacted the prospective teachers' mathematical identities. Adler and Davis (2006) used Bernstein's (1996) educational code theory and Ball and Bass' (2000) notion of "unpacking" in the mathematical work of teaching to study the mathematical knowledge promoted in mathematics courses for teachers in South Africa. In terms of the methodological frameworks, most studies followed the interpretive paradigm with qualitative small-scale approaches (39/59) while the others adopted quantitative (14/59) or mixed methods (6/59).

4 Exploration of PSMT Knowledge

4.1 Large-Scale Projects

Several important large-scale research projects addressed issues of prospective mathematics teacher knowledge in relation to program features. One of these studies is the *Mathematics Teaching in the 21st Century* (MT21) international study that addressed the preparation of middle school mathematics teachers with participation of six countries: South Korea, Taiwan, Bulgaria, Germany, US and Mexico (Schmidt et al. 2011). Regarding mathematics preparation (CK), coursework in linear algebra and calculus and on more advanced mathematics corresponded to higher individual scores (in the two Asian countries) whereas coursework in advanced school mathematics did not. These scores were very much in line with the opportunities to learn (OTL) provided to prospective teachers. For mathematics pedagogy (PCK), only Bulgaria and Mexico had low scores, and the relationship with the OTL was still significant but much lower than regarding CK.

Another project is TEDS-M (Tatto et al. 2010) which surveyed 17 country-regions into the approaches, structures, and characteristics of such programs. The theoretical framework draws on the CK and PCK notions of Shulman (1986). This study is the first international study on mathematics teacher knowledge and offered us important theoretical and methodological perspectives that take into account contextual characteristics of mathematics teacher education in the participating countries (Tatto et al. 2012). Prospective primary and lower secondary teachers' knowledge was assessed through questionnaires including items for testing CK and PCK and general pedagogical knowledge (GPK). There were two different groups of lower secondary teachers, one being prepared to teach up to grade 10 (PG5-Program Group 5) and another being prepared to teach up to grade 11 and above (PG6-Program Group 6).

The TEDS-M main report (Tatto et al. 2012) provides results about several variables, including CK and PCK. Regarding CK, the score of participants from PG6 varied widely, with more than 200 points of difference between the highest and the lowest mean score. Prospective teachers from Taiwan, Russia, Singapore, Germany, and Poland outperformed the participants from the other countries, with a mean score above 559 points (Anchor Point 2). Prospective teachers of PG5 had less variation in their scores with the top performing countries being Singapore, Switzerland, and Poland, with a score above the 500 points (the international mean). Regarding PCK, PG5 participants from Switzerland, Singapore, Poland and Germany had scores above the international mean whereas PG6 participants from Taiwan, Germany, Russia, Singapore, USA, and Poland had scores above 509 (the single Anchor Point).

Blömeke et al. (2013) identified subgroups of countries with specific weaknesses and strengths related to content domains, cognitive demands and item formats. For example, prospective teachers from countries of the East Asia tradition (Taiwan and Singapore) performed better in mathematics content items and in constructed-response items, of the Western tradition (USA, Germany and Norway) did particularly well on data handling and items related to mathematics teaching, and of the Eastern European tradition (Russia and Poland) were strong on non-standard mathematical operations. Blömeke and Delaney (2012) also conducted a literature review of comparative studies in the context of the TEDS-M study discussing its conceptual framework, methodology and main findings. TEDS-M's conceptual and methodological framework measured teacher competences by distinguishing several aspects of teacher knowledge, linking them to beliefs including cognitive and affective dimensions and stressing its situative and applied nature. In addition to the ranking of countries in terms of aspects of prospective teacher knowledge that have already been mentioned above, predictors of teacher knowledge were included. Gender effects (males performed better than females in CK), language effects (teachers whose first language matched the official language of instruction in teacher education performed better both in CK and PCK), prior knowledge (high-school achievement and the number of mathematics classes at school had a positive impact on both CK and PCK) and motivation (subject related motives were positively related both to CK and PCK) were some individual predictors. Institutional predictors, which had a strong influence both on PSMTs' CK and PCK, included opportunities to learn mathematics in teacher education and the quality of teaching method experiences.

Another study that addressed prospective mathematics teachers' knowledge is COACTIV (Krauss et al. 2008). This study sought to establish construct validity for the notions of CK and PCK. The main sample was practicing mathematics teachers ($n = 198$) while prospective secondary school mathematics teachers ($n = 90$) and school students in advanced grade 13 mathematics courses ($n = 30$) were two contrast groups used to validate the instruments. The study concluded that PCK is deeply interrelated with CK and that CK is a prerequisite for PCK. The PCK measure had three subscales, Tasks, Students, and Instruction, with Tasks having the lower correlation to CK. Supporting Shulman's (1986) notion of PCK as an amalgam of CK and GPK, the findings suggest that there are two possible routes to develop PCK, one based on very strong mathematical competence and another based on pedagogical knowledge common to teaching other subjects. It also concluded that prospective mathematics teachers have statistically significant lower CK and PCK regarding gymnasium practicing teachers, albeit not much strong in absolute terms (8.5 vs. 6.6 in CK and 21.0 vs. 18.2 in PCK). It also showed that prospective mathematics teachers significantly outperformed school students in both kinds of knowledge (18.2 vs. 9.7 in PCK and 6.6 vs. 2.6 in CK). This may suggest that both PCK and CK are acquired at university in teacher education programs while their development during the teacher career is not very significant. This reinforces the importance of university and teacher education studies in the development of prospective teachers' knowledge. The COACTIV study was successful in establishing construct validity for CK and PCK as separate notions and suggested that PCK is the most important factor that explains secondary school students' learning (Baumert et al. 2010). However, as Krauss et al. (2008) indicate, its measurement instruments still have room for further improvement, for example, striving to construct PCK items that are not influenced by CK and providing a more suitable representation of geometry items.

4.2 Content-Specific Character of the Research

Studies on PSMT conceptions on specific mathematical concepts in algebra, geometry and statistics, or problem solving/modeling and reasoning/proof indicate that many prospective mathematics teachers for lower and upper secondary education have not developed a deep mathematical knowledge that can inform their teaching towards developing understandings of mathematical concepts and reasoning.

Concerning mathematical concepts, we provide examples of some of these studies addressing the different mathematical areas presented in Table 1. In algebra/numbers, Sirotic and Zazkis (2007) investigated PSMT knowledge of irrational numbers through an analysis of their characteristics (intuitive, algorithmic, formal) and showed inconsistencies between PSMT intuitions and formal and algorithmic knowledge. Caglayan (2013) studied PSMT sense making of polynomial multiplication and factorization modeled with algebra tiles and found three different levels of understanding: additive, one way multiplicative and bidirectional multiplicative. Huang and Kulm (2012) measured PSMT knowledge of algebra for teaching and especially focused on the function concept through a survey instrument aiming to identify PSMT understanding of school and advanced mathematics as well as their views on the teaching of algebra identifying certain limitations in all areas. Alajmi (2015) focused on the algebraic generalization strategies used by PSMTs in linear, exponential and quadratic equations showing that they had difficulties in generalizing algebraic rules especially with exponents, in line with a similar finding from TEDS-M (Tatto et al. 2012).

Yanik (2011) explored PSMTs' knowledge of geometric translations and concluded that PSMT conceived translations mainly as physical motions based on their previous experiences. In calculus, the study of Tsamir et al. (2006) on PSMT images of the concept of derivative and absolute function showed that PSMT gave correct definitions but could not use them appropriately in solving a given task. However, their engagement in evaluating their own responses brought some changes in their initial solutions. Hannigan et al. (2013) focused on conceptual understanding of statistics and the relationship with attitudes towards statistics and found that PSMTs had low conceptual understanding of statistics and positive attitudes, with a low correlation between conceptual understanding and attitudes.

Several studies focused on mathematical processes, problem solving strategies, and modeling. Demircioglu et al. (2010) studied PSMT metacognitive behavior and showed that this behavior was not related to their achievement and type of problems. Regarding modeling, all the papers focused on the construction of mathematical models by PSMT. Daher and Shahbari (2015) showed different ways of how technology was integrated in the modeling process. Delice and Kertil (2015) also looked for PSMT connections of the modeling process to different forms of representations, and indicated difficulties of PSMTs in making such connections. Carrejo and Marshall (2007) investigated the modeling process in the context of a physics course and showed that PSMTs began to question the nature of mathematics in their attempt to make connections to the real world. The study of Eli et al. (2011) also focused on the mathematical connections that PSMTs made while engaged in card-sorting activities and found that most of the PSMTs' connections were procedural and categorical.

Reasoning and proof was also the focus of some papers. Yenem-Karpuzcu et al. (2015) studied PSMT covariational reasoning abilities showing different levels for low and high achievers. Zazkis and Zazkis (2015) used PSMT scripted dialogues between teacher and students related to the proof of Pythagoras' theorem to address how they comprehend students' understanding of proof showing that PSMTs mostly considered errors on algebraic manipulations and did not assess proof comprehension in a holistic way. Stylianides et al. (2007) studied PSMT knowledge on mathematical induction, identifying certain difficulties on the essence of the base step of the induction method, the meaning of the inductive step, and the possibility of the truth set of a statement proved by mathematical induction to include values outside its domain of discourse. Corleis et al. (2008) examined PSMTs' CK and PCK about argumentation and proof in Germany and Hong Kong and indicated that PSMTs from Hong Kong performed better in their CK about proof and argumentation than those from Germany, while there was no difference in PCK.

4.3 Relation of PSMT Knowledge to Teaching

A number of studies focused on the relationship between PSMTs' CK and PCK showing rather positive relations. Van den Kieboom et al. (2014) reported that PSMTs' algebraic proficiency was related to the questions that they asked while interviewing students. Positive relations also were reported in the studies of Karp (2010), Charalambus (2015) and Mamolo and Pali (2014). Whereas the study of Karp (2010) showed that lack of PCK creates difficulties in PSMT field experiences, the study of Morris et al. (2009) focused on how PSMT unpack learning goals into subconcepts and found that although PSMTs identified such subconcepts they could not use them in the context of teaching. Similarly, Johnson et al. (2014) found that the PSMT's use of definitions and examples while doing mathematics did not seem to influence their teaching. Magiera et al. (2013) also reported that PSMTs' algebraic thinking and its relation to the analysis of tasks and students' algebraic thinking were not smoothly related. The study of Capraro et al. (2012) on problem solving also showed that mathematical competence does not translate to pedagogical effectiveness. Finally, the study of Subramaniam (2014) examined PSMT PCK for teaching the estimation of length measurement by examining their personal benchmarks and showed that holding mathematical knowledge does not guarantee knowledge for teaching.

4.4 *Epistemological and Theoretical Issues*

Three papers focus on epistemological and theoretical issues related to PSMT knowledge. Moreira and David (2008) addressed the differences between school and academic mathematics knowledge related to number systems pointing out that mathematics teacher educators need to be aware of these differences. Speer, King and Howell (2015) discussed the relevance of frameworks of studying mathematics teacher knowledge at the primary level up to the secondary and college level. They argued that frameworks for primary teachers have to be extended, as there are differences in the nature of knowledge required for secondary and college mathematics teachers. Koirala et al. (2008) developed an assessment performance task and rubric to measure PCK based on the analysis of students' needs and on the design of lesson plans.

5 Impact of Teacher Education Practices on PSMT Knowledge

The impact of teacher education programs on PSMT knowledge has been studied both in the large-scale studies TEDS-M and COACTIV and in small-scale studies. TEDS-M (in Li 2012) shows that there is difficulty on making direct connections between teachers' performance and their program of studies even within an education system (e.g. in Singapore). However, in the case of the US, it appears that selecting more mathematically able students in teacher education and providing key mathematics and mathematics pedagogy opportunities to learn in the courses, has a positive impact on the development of PSMT knowledge. The study of Wang and Tang (2013) uses the data from TEDS-M and analyses the opportunities to learn (OTL) offered in the context of teacher education programs for prospective secondary mathematics teachers in fifteen countries. The results show that three profiles of OTL appear at tertiary-level mathematics, school-level mathematics, mathematics education and general education. Tertiary-level mathematics demand extensive and intensive coverage of topics, Mathematics education courses focus more on students' cognitive understandings and abilities while general education emphasizes the relation to school practice and the comprehensive coverage of topics. In the case of COACTIV study and in particular in the context of COACTIV-R study that focused on professional competences of prospective teacher, it appears that offering formal learning opportunities at the teacher education level promotes PSMT knowledge (Kunter et al. 2013). Through the small-scale studies, different teacher education practices seem to promote PSMT knowledge. One of them is PSMT engagement in tasks with certain characteristics. Zbiek and Conner (2006) argued that PSMT engagement in modeling tasks indicates changes in PSMT motivation and understanding of the modeling process. The study of Stankey and Sundstrom (2007) showed how a high school task can be extended to teacher education while the study of Levenson (2013) focused on the process of selecting and analyzing tasks related to mathematical creativity showing that PSMT take into account not only features and cognitive demands in their analysis and choices but also affective factors. Steele et al. (2013) suggested that the connection between CCK and SCK can be developed through PSMT engagement with rich tasks first as learners, sharing solutions, and then analyzing the tasks as teachers.

There are studies referring to instructional sequences in teacher education that appear to be effective in developing PSMT CK. Bleiler et al. (2014) proposed an instructional sequence to improve PSMT proof validation of students' arguments in number theory. The sequence consists of five activities including marking students' responses to proof tasks, analyzing a video extract of a teacher facing a student's inductive argument, discussing in groups, and validating proof arguments provided by students in other research studies, grading individually students' proof arguments, justifying the score, and providing feedback to the students. However, their findings do not show any change in PSMT proof validation before and after the teacher education course. Similarly, Moon et al. (2013) referred to a three-week teaching unit designed to overcome PSMTs' difficulties in understanding the big ideas related to connections among representations in the context of conic curves showing that PSMTs had difficulties relating to the variation, the Cartesian connection, and graphs as locus of points. Prediger (2010) suggested a number of teacher education strategies that support the development of PSMT diagnostic competence in algebra (e.g., evaluating students' and their peers' responses).

Adler and Davis (2006), Hossin et al. (2013), and Adler et al. (2014) refer to a mathematics enhancement program. Adler and Davis (2006) reported findings from a survey of teacher education programs in South Africa that aimed to develop PSMT CK and show that the mathematics taught was compressed without promoting mathematical ideas and reasoning. Hossin et al. (2013) studied the impact of this course on the development of PSMT mathematical and teaching identity and identified several issues with the course regarding the process of developing mathematics teachers. Adler et al. (2014) indicated that PSMT conceived "understanding mathematics in depth" because of their participation in this course showing that their conceptions were influenced by the way that mathematics was considered in the course.

Some studies focus mainly on teacher education strategies that support PSMT to develop PCK or pedagogical knowledge. Viseu and Ponte (2012) showed the impact of a course that integrates the use of ICT tools (emails and forum) on the development of a PSMT planning and teaching. The PSMT started to use tasks that are more open and initiated more productive classroom communication. Jenkins (2010) showed that PSMT advanced their PCK by being engaged in preparing task-based interviews, doing and analyzing the interviews, preparing a report linking their findings to the research discussed in the course, and sharing this with their peers. Sanchez-Matamoros et al. (2014) described a teaching module aimed to promote PSMT noticing of students' thinking of the derivative of a function through a number of different tasks such as analyzing students' work and solving problems themselves. The module focuses on the learning trajectory of the derivative concept and the findings show that it had a positive impact on PSMT noticing of students' thinking. Aguirre et al. (2012) focused on the process of supporting PSMT to develop PCK by taking into account cultural and social issues. The designed course and the assignment given to PSMT asked them to analyze their own teaching by using categories that also address culturally responsive characteristics. Although PSMT were receptive to these approaches, they did not develop the pedagogical ways of addressing them into their teaching.

A number of studies investigated ways of developing both CK and PCK. Groth and Bergner (2013) focused on the development of CK and PCK in statistics and in particular in analyzing categorical data. The activities in which they engaged PSMT were analyzing themselves data and reading papers about learning and teaching categorical analysis. They showed that various types of knowledge structures developed through the analysis of PSMT writing prompts from their readings and the analysis of students' errors. Clark (2012) showed a positive impact of a history of mathematics course designed to show the development of mathematics, the cultural and historical influences and the integration of history in teaching on PSMT development of mathematical and pedagogical awareness. Tsamir (2005) introduced PSMT to the theory of intuitive rules and showed development of PSMT CK and PCK. The PSMT were asked to construct intuitive and counter intuitive tasks about "same A–same B" and report episodes that they identified in their practicum analyzing them by using this theory. Finally, Davis (2009) showed that reading and planning of PSMT from two different textbooks had a positive impact on PSMT CK and PCK of exponential function.

6 The Process of PSMT Knowledge Development in the Context of Teacher Education Programs

Few studies focus on the actual process of PSMT development in the actual teacher education program analyzing interactions in order to trace teacher knowledge at mathematical and pedagogical level. Ticknor (2012) investigated whether PSMTs who participate in an abstract algebra course made links with high school algebra by relating individual's mathematical history to the community of the classroom of the course and vice versa and concluded that such links are not easy. Assuming mathematical creativity as a component to teacher knowledge, Shriki (2010) addressed how it can be developed in a context of a methods course. The PSMT initially focused on the creative product considering mathematics as a closed domain while later in the course they focused on the creative process viewing mathematics as an open domain. Tsamir (2007) analyzed a lesson in a teacher education course focusing on psychological aspects of mathematics education and in particular on the role of intuitive rules in learning. Her main finding is that intuitive rules acted as a tool for supporting PSMT reflection on their own methods and intuitive solutions. Ryve et al. (2012) addressed how mathematics teacher educators establish "mathematics for teaching" in teacher education programs by using variation theory to analyze classroom interaction in a teacher education course. Parker and Adler (2014) studied knowledge and practice in mathematics teacher education focusing on both knowledge of mathematics and knowledge of mathematics teaching and their co-constitution. They recognize shifts between mathematics and mathematics teaching but claim that the recognition and realization rules for the privileged text (using Bernstein's theory of pedagogic discourse) with respect to mathematics teaching were available.

7 Final Remarks

Research continues to show that the PSMT knowledge of mathematical content and processes is plagued with difficulties and low conceptual understanding of many concepts. However, the studies do not stem from a common framework regarding what must be required from prospective secondary teachers, and requirements established by researchers seems to vary in nature and depth. In this area, an important step forward would be the establishment of such frameworks (as suggested by Speer et al. 2015) and a common understanding of important steps in the development in PSMT mathematical knowledge (learning frameworks). Concerning knowledge of mathematics teaching, didactical knowledge or PCK, we seem to have an even more precarious situation, given the scarce number of studies in the field and the fuzziness that still accompanies this notion. As the work of Kaarstein (2015) showed, PCK is an elusive notion, and its distinction of mathematics knowledge is often problematic. The large-scale national and international studies on teacher knowledge also point towards a very complex relation between PCK and CK.

   The studies on the impact of teacher education practices and the processes of how PSMT knowledge develops in teacher education programs suggest that the active engagement of participants in doing mathematics and discussing strategies and results has a positive influence in their mathematics learning. In addition, PSMT active engagement in preparing tasks, analyzing students' work, giving feedback to students, and discussing with colleagues and teacher educators are also positive influences on their knowledge about mathematics teaching. Looking closely at students' thinking is a major trend in the research carried out in the last ten years and may have an important impact on PSMT learning. When they are in fieldwork placements, ICT may be a useful means for communication and interaction. For dealing with specific topics, we will probably need local theories that indicate what kinds of tasks, materials and environments promote a stronger development. Moreover, taking into account the complexity of mathematics teaching, we need to extend our teacher education practices into directions so that this complexity becomes transparent to PSMT. Addressing complexity in teacher education challenges researchers and educators to consider PSMT knowledge and its development under new more participatory theoretical perspectives.

Besides the focus on knowledge, we also need to strengthen the focus on how PSMT develop knowledge (Cochran-Smith and Villegas 2015). There are already a good number of studies giving hints on how this may occur in specific courses within university contexts. However, we also need to know how PSMT PCK is fostered through their practicum or in other kinds of fieldwork, since field placements are dubbed as powerful settings for the development of PSMT knowledge in all of its dimensions.

Chapter 3
Prospective Secondary Mathematics Teacher Preparation and Technology

Rongjin Huang and Rose Mary Zbiek

1 Introduction

Practitioners and researchers interested in prospective secondary mathematics teacher (PSMT) preparation can see technology as both an object of PSMT learning and a means for that learning. In this chapter, we present a systematic review of empirical literature to describe how PSMTs benefit from technology use in teacher preparation.

To arrive at the set of references, the first author searched each of nine core mathematics education journals for articles published between 2000 and 2015 using key words: "technology", "pre-service" or "prospective", and "secondary mathematics teachers". Abstracts, theoretical backgrounds and methodology sections indicated 25 articles that reported empirical results. A search of six refereed journals focused on technology, mathematics education, or teacher education[1] for articles published between 2000 and 2015 using "secondary mathematics teachers" and either "pre-service" or "prospective" as key words. Upon careful reading the 35 articles, we selected 18 that focused on prospective secondary mathematics teachers and reported an empirical study.

---

[1]International Journal for Technology in Mathematics Education, International Journal of Mathematical Education in Science and Technology, Journal of Technology and Teacher Education, Contemporary Issues in Technology and Teacher Education, Journal of Research on Technology in Education, Journal of Digital Learning in Teacher Education.

R. Huang (✉)
Department of Mathematical Sciences, Middle Tennessee State University, Murfreesboro, TN, USA
e-mail: rhuang@mtsu.edu

R.M. Zbiek
College of Education, The Pennsylvania State University, University Park, PA, USA
e-mail: rmz101@psu.edu

© The Author(s) 2017
M.E. Strutchens et al., *The Mathematics Education of Prospective Secondary Teachers Around the World*, ICME-13 Topical Surveys,
DOI 10.1007/978-3-319-38965-3_3

We observed that the articles could be sorted into three categories based on contexts of PSMT preparation in which the empirical work occurred: (1) mathematics content courses; (2) methods or pedagogy courses; and (3) teaching practicum. Within each venue, we note trends and questions regarding the PMSTs' experiences with technology. All reviewed articles addressed, either explicitly or implicitly, knowledge about content, pedagogy, technology, or interactions or combinations thereof.

2 Framing Knowledge and Course Redesign

Knowledge about content, pedagogy, technology, and combinations of these areas might be framed by Technological, Pedagogical and Content Knowledge (TPACK). TPACK refers to the knowledge on which teachers rely for teaching content with appropriate digital technologies (Koehler and Mishra 2008; Mishra and Koehler 2006). Built upon Shulman's (1986) ideas, the structure of knowledge associated with TPACK includes three major components of knowledge: content knowledge, pedagogical knowledge and technological knowledge. The model "emphasizes the complex interplay of these three bodies of knowledge" (Koehler and Mishra 2008, p. 1025) with Shulman's pedagogical content knowledge (PCK) and the introduction of technological pedagogical knowledge (TPK), technological content knowledge (TCK), and technological pedagogical content knowledge (TPACK).

Niess (2012) argued that those preparing teachers for meeting the challenges and demands for teaching mathematics with appropriate 21st century digital technologies must address the question of how pre-service teachers' preparation programs should be re-designed to describe appropriate learning trajectories for learning to teach mathematics in the 21st century. A redesigned course or practicum should engage pre-service teachers with rich pedagogical, technological, and content problems, maintaining the complexity of the interrelationships among these bodies of knowledge. Within the following discussion of content courses, pedagogy courses, and practicum, redesign of experiences provides the context and motivation of several empirical works.

3 Content Courses and Technologies

Four articles examined whether various technologies could be used to promote PSMTs' understanding of mathematics content (Cory and Carofal 2011), increase their performance in mathematics content (Kopran 2015; Zengin and Tatar 2015), or change their attitudes toward using technology in teaching and learning mathematics (Halat 2009; Kopran 2015; Zengin and Tatar 2015).

Findings from three of the studies (Cory and Carolal 2009; Halat 2009; Zengin and Tatar 2015) suggest PSMTs' use of dynamic environment or interactive technology might help them develop a better understanding of the content. These results arose across mathematics content, including limits of sequences (Cory and Carolal 2009), polar coordinates (Zengin and Tatar 2015), and statistics (Kopran 2015). Researchers employing qualitative methods (Cory and Carolal 2009; Zengin and Tatar 2015) explored conceptual understanding while work using quantitative methods (Kopran 2015) focused on comparisons of performance. Use of such constructs as concept image (Tall and Vinner 1981) might be helpful in articulating how the technology use contributed to richer content knowledge.

Three studies indicated that use of dynamic software (Halat 2009; Zengin and Tatar 2015) or interactive, web-based learning tool and resources (Kopran 2015) could develop participants' positive attitudes toward teaching and learning mathematics with technologies. For example, PSMTs involved in Koparan's (2015) study showed positive attitude toward learning statistics, perhaps identifying the technology as interesting and useful tools for data processing. Halat (2011) examined the effects of PSMTs designing a Webquest, a computer-based learning and teaching model in which learners are actively involved in an activity or situation and use the Internet as a resource. His participants' attitudes and perceptions changed as they noted the usefulness of Webquest for motiving students and assessing students' learning, and promoting students' collaboration.

4   Pedagogy or Methods Courses and Technologies

Thirteen articles examined how to develop PSMTs' understanding through pedagogy or methods courses. Each of the studies addressed technology in combination with one or both of content and pedagogy.

Only one of the 13 articles addresses pedagogy. Zembat (2008) examined the nature of mathematical reasoning and algebraic thinking in a paper-and-pencil environment compared to that in a technology-supported environment (Sketchpad and Graphing calculators). He used Sternberg's (1999) model to describe three types of reasoning:

> Analytical reasoning refers to the ability to think about formulas and applications of those to abstract mathematical problems that usually have single correct answers. ... Practical reasoning refers to the ability to solve everyday problems or reason about applications. ... Creative reasoning refers to the invention of methods in thinking about problems. (p. 146)

Four interview participants' solving of optimization problems indicated that, within a paper-and-pencil environment, they depended on and were limited to analytical reasoning. However, they were able to exhibit analytical, practical, and creative reasoning with the help of the facilities that technology environments provided. This finding connects to our observation in Sect. 3.3 that dynamic environments or interactive technology might help PSMTs develop better understanding of content. Either practical and creative reasoning might help PSMTs develop deeper understanding or these forms of reasoning and development of deeper understanding depend on a common type of interaction with technology among successful PSMTs.

Six articles explored pedagogical ideas. They differ regarding whether they explore the use of video or the use of mathematics software, though all addressed some aspects of teacher questioning. Akkoc (2015) examined formative assessment skills within a computer-learning environment (e.g., GeoGebra, TI Nspire). Analysis of 35 PSMTs' pre- and post-workshop lesson plans and teaching notes indicated that participants improved their mathematical questioning regarding mathematical reasoning, assessment of prior knowledge, connections, and multiple representations, and they dramatically increased their use of questions assessing technical aspects of using technology. Davis (2015) investigated how 10 PSMTs read, evaluated, and adapted elements of a textbook lesson involving symbolic manipulation capabilities of computer algebra systems (CAS). A majority of the PSMTs adapted lessons to ask students to make predictions before using CAS and helping students understand the hidden procedures used by the technology but did not necessarily connect lesson elements to overarching lesson goals. These studies might suggest ways to improve teacher questioning yet underscore the challenge of coordinating questioning with other lesson aspects. They suggest how PSMTs might progress in some ways, regardless of their mathematical ability, but need additional support to apply knowledge in practice.

Arguably one of the most robust bodies of literature emerging around the use of technology in PSMT education regards the use of video in methods courses. However, researchers attend to different aspects of teaching episodes. For example, Santagata et al. (2007) examined how a video-based method course can develop PSMTs' ability in analyzing lessons guided by a three-step analysis framework that values goals and parts of the lesson, student learning, and teaching alternatives. Open-ended pre- and post-assessments from 140 participants revealed improved analysis. Taking a more targeted approach, Star and Strickland (2007) investigated how video use in a methods course could help develop PSMTs' noticing ability. Twenty-eight PSMTs' pre- and post-tests documented quantity and types of classroom events that teachers noticed before and after the course. After the pre-assessment, a multi-dimension framework (environment, management, tasks, content, and communication) was used to guide students' analyzing of videos throughout the course. The data analysis revealed that, although the PSMT generally lacked observational skills, they enhanced their skills in noticing important features of the classroom environment, mathematical content of a lesson, and teacher and student communication during a lesson. Moreover, Alsawaie and Alghazo (2010) conducted a quasi-experiment on the effect of using video lesson analysis on PSMTs' ability to analyze mathematics teaching. With 26 PSMTs participating in a quasi-experiment, the intervention seemingly remarkably improved participants' ability to analyze classroom teaching. These three studies support use of video and guided discussion to develop various PSMTs' noticing abilities.

In contrast to those interested in questioning and noticing, Rhine and colleagues (2015) investigated PSMT dispositions in a deliberately designed methods course that focused on developing ability to anticipate students' engagement with algebra using multiple integrated technological approaches (e.g., student thinking video database, class response system, and virtual manipulatives). Findings within a mixed methods design using a disposition survey indicated an impact on orientation toward student thinking and efforts to anticipate students' experience of the mathematics. The authors recognized the complexity of assessing disposition and a need for a longitudinal study to determine the effectiveness of using the combined technological resources. Evidence across the six studies shows the potential of using various technological tools and resources for developing PSMTs' mathematical reasoning, algebraic thinking, questioning skills, noticing ability, as well as challenges and complexities.

Acting as teachers in hypothetical situations in which students are using technology, PSMTs seem challenged in facilitating reasoning and problem solving. For example, Hähkiöniemi and Leppäaho (2011) examined how PSMTs guided students' reasoning in hypothetical situations where students were solving inquiry tasks with GeoGebra. Twenty PSMTs explored situations with GeoGebra then wrote their responses as teachers to the students' solutions. The authors concluded that participants had difficulties in guiding students to justify observations, in reacting to trial-and-error solution methods, and in elaborating on unexpected potentially productive ideas.

Eliciting thinking was also a challenge noted by Lee (2005), who examined how three PSMTs interpreted and developed in their role of facilitating students' problem solving with technologies (e.g., dynamic geometry, spreadsheets, probability simulators). A cycle of planning-experience-reflection was repeated twice to allow PSMTs to change strategies when they worked with two different groups of students. Case study methods revealed that the PSMTs desired to ask questions that would guide students in their solution strategies but recognized their own struggles in facilitating students' problem solving. In fact, the PSMTs assumed the role of an explainer for some portion of their work with students. However, they used technological representations to promote students' mathematical thinking or focus their attention.

Seemingly fundamental to facilitation of student reasoning and problem solving is anticipating and eliciting student thinking. Lee and Hollebrands (2008) developed mathematics methods course materials and situations based on enhanced capabilities of the technology to prepare teachers to teach data analysis and probability topics. They developed video cases focusing on enhancing PSMTs' knowledge of students' thinking as they were learning about data analysis within technology-enhanced environments. The 15 participants in pilot tests of the materials seemingly improved in their understanding of statistical and probabilistic concepts and their use of technological tools but not in their pedagogical understandings. Findings resulting from Wilson et al. (2011) extensive analysis of sixteen PSMTs' work on the video-case and student work with technology indicated that reflection on the video case materials provide opportunities for PSMTs' building models of students' thinking.

The studies cited in this section provide evidence that redesigning methods courses to have PSMTs working with dynamic mathematics environments might be productive but PSMTs' struggles to facilitate students' reasoning and problem solving are nontrivial. Reflection with video cases could enhance PSMTs' understanding and anticipation of student thinking, which seems essential in using technology to support students' reasoning and problem solving. Haciomeroglu et al. (2010) shared similarly positive findings about effective lesson development and positive influence on perspectives about teaching and learning of mathematics with technology given use of GeoGebra in a methods course. However, as Haciomeroglu et al. (2010) note, PSMTs' lack of teaching experience remains an issue.

Insight into the connection between preparatory courses and classroom teaching performance might come from Meagher et al. (2011). They examined PSMTs' evolving attitudes regarding the use of various digital technologies (TI-Nspire) in the context of the interplay between their field placements and their use of technologies in inquiry-based lessons. Their 22 PSMTs enrolled in a mathematics teaching methods course that included two field experiences. Several products arose from their analysis of data: a mathematics technology attitude survey; three short surveys regarding philosophy of teaching; experiences with technology in the class; the interactions among the class, mathematics content, technology, and field placement; an open-ended exit survey; and five lesson plans. First, if PSMTs are to develop a positive attitude toward technology use in their instructional practice, more than a methods class is required. In particular, modeling of exemplary practice in the field placement has a crucial, perhaps decisive, effect on their attitudes. Second, the most significant improvement in the quality of the PSMTs' lesson plans regarding inquiry-based teaching with technology came when they had field placements in technology-rich environments.

5 Teacher Practicum and Technologies

Two articles examined PSMTs using technology during student teaching, which is arguably the richest field experience in a PSMT's preparation. A contrast of the two articles is informative.

Fraser et al. (2011) investigated effects of use of technology (e.g., Sketchpad, SMART board) by 16 PSMTs in a technology-rich, five-year teacher education program on lesson planning and quality of classroom life. Pre- and post-placement interviews and five 90-min teaching episodes with debriefings, weekly reflective journals, and lesson artifacts evidenced PSMTs' views of planning, effective mathematics teaching, potential benefits of technology, and motives for using technology. One of the findings was that PMSTs refocused their teaching when they were diverted from their plans.

In methodological contrast to Fraser and colleagues, Clarke (2009) presented a case study of how a PSMT experienced and perceived technology use during student teaching practice. The teacher had expertise in using technologies (TI-83 plus) and was interested in implementing a learner-centered approach through integrating technology. He did not achieve this goal. The author raised a broad concern about provision of necessary resources, support, and professional development.

6   What Do We Know and What Do We Need to Know

The preceding literature review suggests three positive conclusions. First, four studies suggests that engagement with interactive, dynamic tools could enhance PSMTs' understanding of subject knowledge and develop their positive attitudes toward using technologies in their further teaching. Much remains unknown about how to develop and implement materials and initiatives to help PSMTs develop and employ knowledge. For example, although positive outcomes in using video cases in methods courses are documented, specifics of how to develop and use high-quality video cases need to be further explored (Borko et al. 2014).

Second, incorporation of mathematics technology and practice-based video cases in teaching methods courses could help PSMTs in questioning and lesson planning and in anticipating, noticing, and eliciting student thinking. Incorporating technologies in mathematics and methods courses and connecting courses with field experiences could promote PSMTs' awareness of implementing student-centered mathematics instruction and help them identify as technology innovators.

Third, perhaps PSMTs' progress in facilitating student thinking, reasoning, and problem solving seemed elusive. It also could be a sign for long-term studies of development. The ability to notice and elicit student thinking might need to be minially established before teachers can be expected to succeed in eliciting and examining and facilitate student reasoning and problem solving.

Preparing PSMTs to teach secondary mathematics with technology is an important endeavor and an emerging research area in need of systematic studies and a global effort to develop a cohesive body of literature.

Chapter 4
Current Research on Prospective Secondary Mathematics Teachers' Professional Identity

Leticia Losano and Márcia Cristina de Costa Trindade Cyrino

1 Introduction

Identity is a construct widely investigated in a number of research fields and has a variety of interpretations. It is a relevant area of study within mathematics teacher education research (Skott et al. 2013), and several researchers have used it as a theoretical lens (Brown and McNamara 2011; Gama and Fiorentini 2008; Oliveira 2004; Ponte and Chapman 2008; Pamplona and Carvalho 2009; Walshaw 2004, 2010). In this survey we analyzed research studies related to the professional identities of prospective secondary mathematics teachers (PSMTs).

According to Sachs (2005), "teacher professional identity stands at the core of the teaching profession. It provides a framework for teachers to construct their own ideas of 'how to be', 'how to act' and 'how to understand' their work and their place in society" (p. 15). Teacher professional identity is a complex notion since it addresses the complex and mutual relationships between the teachers, the institutions where they work, and the societies where they live. In this way, professional identity is a notion that gathers together personal and social aspects, encompassing knowledge and beliefs, emotions and relationships, and context and experiences (Van Putten et al. 2014). Professional identities are developed collectively with others, in the interactions a teacher has with school principals, colleagues, students, parents, etc. Although professional identity involves what others think or say about a person, it also involves how a person sees herself, her capacity to reflect upon her experiences, and her capacity to act upon the world for creating new ways of being.

L. Losano (✉)
Universidad Nacional de Córdoba, Córdoba, Argentina
e-mail: losano@famaf.unc.edu.ar

M.C. de Costa Trindade Cyrino
Universidade Estadual de Londrina, Londrina, Brazil
e-mail: marciacyrino@uel.br

M.E. Strutchens et al., *The Mathematics Education of Prospective Secondary Teachers Around the World*, ICME-13 Topical Surveys,
DOI 10.1007/978-3-319-38965-3_4

In this way, professional identity development is also intrinsically related to the development of agency.

Therefore, the PSMTs' identity development is a complex process that includes the personal, professional, intellectual, moral, and political dimensions of prospective teachers and the groups in which they are involved (Beijaard et al. 2004; Day et al. 2005; Kelchtermans 2009; Lasky 2005; Oliveira and Cyrino 2011). The future oriented dimension of professional identities is especially important for PSMT's education. As Beijaard et al. (2004) pointed out, professional identities are not "only an answer to the question 'Who am I at this moment?', but also an answer to the question, 'Who do I want to become?'" (p. 122). Thus, analyzing how PSMTs construct their identities in the spaces and moments offered and promoted by pre-service education is an important issue.

2 Methodology of the Survey

In agreement with other members of the survey topic group, the authors sought studies related to PSMTs' professional identity that were published in the nine international research journals in mathematics education and two relevant Latin-American journals.[1] The researchers felt that including the two Latin-American journals in the search would enable them to capture research that has been conducted by mathematics educators from non-English-speaking countries.

The review of the literature was restricted to the period from 2005 to 2015.[2] Several searches were conducted using combinations of the key words "prospective teachers" and "secondary" with the following key words related to professional identity: "identity", "self", and "agency". For each search result, the article's title and abstract were read. If the study was connected to professional identity, then it was selected. Several studies were excluded that addressed the notion of identity, but were focused on students, prospective elementary mathematics teachers, in service mathematics teachers, or mathematics educators. Consequently, some of the targeted journals did not include studies, which met our criteria. This search resulted in the selection of 14 articles.

Next, the articles were read and analyzed with respect to their (1) focus, (2) theoretical perspective, (3) methodology, and (4) findings. The analysis of the articles led to a division of the studies into two groups. Group 1 is comprised of four articles, which do not address professional identity directly, but they focus on important related notions. These notions are *field/habitus and dispositions* (Nolan

---

[1]*Bolema* (Boletim de Educação Matemática—Mathematics Education Bulletin) edited by the São Paulo University (UNESP) and *Relime* (Revista Latinoamericana de Matemática Educativa—Latin-American Journal of Mathematics Education) edited by the Latin-American Committee of Mathematics Education.

[2]It is important to highlight that the survey was carried out in November, 2015. In this way, the last volumes of the year 2015 were not considered.

2012), *beliefs about the teacher's role* (Lloyd 2005), *narrative writing* (Gonçalves and De Carvalho 2014), and *emotionality* (Boylan 2010).

Group 2 is comprised of 10 studies in which professional identity is the main focus of the research. In each of these studies, the notion of identity is mentioned in at least one of the research questions or is the main aim of the research. In addition, these studies conceptualize, in diverse ways and degrees, the notion of identity and present findings related to PSMTs' professional identity. The review shows that the number of studies focused on PSMTs' professional identity is growing over time which made it possible to find studies in the selected journals from the period of 2005–2015. *JMTE* and *ESM* are the journals which have published most of the research reports focused on this topic during the period considered. The ten articles were separated into three sub-groups based mainly on their research focus: (a) studies that addressed the relationships between PSMTs' identities and field experiences during pre-service education, (b) studies centered on the linkages between PSMTs' identities and the learning of specific mathematical topics, and (c) studies that investigated the ways in which PSMTs represented their professional identity. In the following section, we describe each sub-group by summarizing the articles that compose them.

3   The Selected Studies: What Has Been Studied in the Area?

3.1   Professional Identity and Field Experiences

Four studies addressed the relationships between the development of a professional identity and field experiences during prospective secondary mathematics teacher education programs. Goos (2005) analyzed the personal and contextual factors that influenced the development of PSMTs' pedagogical identities. This study considers the transition from pre-service education to beginning teaching of secondary school mathematics and investigates PSMTs' experiences during practicum and during their first year of serving as mathematics teachers in schools. Particularly, the author focused on the part of the PSMTs' pedagogical identity concerned with technology use. The authorshowed that PSMTs develop their identities by "negotiating changing relationships between their teaching environments, their actions, and their beliefs" (p. 54). Thus, this study highlighted that PSMTs are active agents that re-interpret the social conditions of the practicum environment in the light of their own professional goals and beliefs.

Goos and Bennison (2008) focused on the notion of communal identity as they investigated the PSMTs' sense of connectedness and belonging in relation to an online community of practice (CoP). Two successive cohorts of PSMTs enrolled in a mathematics curriculum course participated in this CoP, which included the PSMTs sending, reading, and answering messages on a bulletin board. The authors found that the CoP's joint enterprise of becoming a mathematics teacher was defined differently as the PSMTs moved between the university and professional contexts. In the university context, the negotiated enterprise was related to the practice of being a university student. In the professional context (which includes practicum) the enterprise was related to the practice of teaching in the school.

Van Putten et al. (2014) also addressed the relationships between PSMTs' identities and the teaching practicum, but in a different light. These authors investigated the professional mathematics teacher identity in terms of the relationships between the PSMTs' self-perceived identity and the PSMTs' actualized identity in the classroom during practicum. The authors considered that PSMTs develop their professional mathematics teacher identity from their perceptions of themselves as mathematics specialists, as teaching-and-learning specialists, and as caring specialists. The main result of this study was the existence of incongruences between PSMTs' perceptions of their identity and the actualization of that identity in the classroom, particularly in terms of their perceptions as teaching-and-learning specialists and as caring specialists.

The fourth article, written by Teixeira and Cyrino (2015), is focused on the role that the planning stage plays in the development of some aspects of PSMTs' professional identities before the teaching practicum. The authors investigated the interactions between PSMTs and their university supervisors during planning meetings. Teixeira and Cyrino (2015) concluded that the interactions promoted by university supervisors who held a "questioning attitude" led to the development of several elements related to the PSMTs' professional identities, such as the awakening of a critical sense in planning lessons, the development of an inquiry attitude, and the ability to reflect on the lesson plans before teaching the lessons.

3.2 PSMTs' Identities and the Learning of Specifics Mathematical Topics

Three of the four studies that constituted this group investigated the relationships between the development of PSMTs' identities and the learning of specific mathematical topics during pre-service education. In the fourth study the researchers sought to develop a theoretical framework for investigating a particularly situated identity of mathematics teachers: their identity as embedders-of-numeracy.

Gonçalves Costa and Pamplona (2011) analyzed the opportunities that pre-service education offers to PSMTs for developing their identities as statistical educators. Drawing on a situated learning perspective, the authors used the notion of participation in CoPs for describing and analyzing the curricular transformation of a mathematics education degree program. This study highlighted that in order for PSMTs to assume identities as statistical educators, it is necessary to introduce modifications in the curriculum of mathematics education degree programs including courses that cross boundaries between mathematical, statistical, pedagogical, and professional practices.

Ticknor (2012) also made use of the notion of participation in CoPs and combined it with the person-in-practice-in-person (Lerman 2001) unit of analysis. With these analytical tools Ticknor (2012) explored how PSMTs' mathematical identities were influenced by their participation in a CoP developed inside an abstract algebra course. Ticknor (2012) claimed that observing the instructor's teaching style had an impact on the PSMTs' identities, which might have influenced the PSMTs' pedagogical approaches.

Drawing on Badiou's and Lacan's theories, Brown et al. (2013) sought to analyze how PSMTs "variously identify with particular conceptions of mathematics and how those identifications support teacher education ambitions" (p. 56). The authors analyzed a set of episodes, which occurred during sessions with PSMTs devoted to the apprehension of mathematical objects through exercises centered on the PSMTs' own bodily movements. The authors showed that the PSMTs narratives of their process of emerging understanding documented human subjects and mathematical objects coming into being. In this way, "in becoming teachers they are participating in the becoming of mathematics" (p. 571).

Bennison's (2015) article also addressed professional identity development, but in relation to the notion of numeracy. The author constructed a theoretical framework looking at characteristics of identity that seemed particularly relevant for the "context of teachers promoting growth in the numeracy capabilities of students through the subjects they teach" (p. 9). Reviewing the literature, Bennison (2015) proposed a theoretical framework built around five domains of influence: the knowledge domain, the affective domain, the social domain, the life story domain, and the context domain. Although the development of this theoretical framework was not focused solely on PSMTs, the study was included in the survey because several research questions related to PSMTs' identities as embedders of numeracy can be addressed with the framework.

3.3   PSMTs Representing Their Professional Identity

Two articles investigated the ways in which PSMTs represented their professional identity. The first one addressed the issue by analyzing written PSMTs' fictional accounts of mathematics classrooms (Lloyd 2006), and the second one examined the issue by investigating how PSMTs use, and are used, by the dominant discourses of a mathematics enhancement course (Houssain et al. 2013).

Lloyd (2006) studied professional identity in terms of how it is represented by PSMTs' written fictional accounts of mathematics classrooms. The study results showed that the PSMTs' emerging identities represented in their fictional accounts altered the traditional classroom roles for students and teachers. Thus, PSMTs' stories represented inquiry-oriented classrooms where the teacher sets up the content and structure of mathematics activities for students to investigate and discuss. Once the students began to work on these activities, the teacher's role became less apparent. Lloyd's (2006) study underlined that defining the role of the teacher in an inquiry-oriented classroom is an issue that remains open for many—particularly for PSMTs.

Hossain et al. (2013) explored the notion of PSMTs' professional identity through a poststructuralist lens. They focused on a Mathematics Enhancement Course developed in order to prepare non-mathematics graduates to train as secondary mathematics teachers. In this study, the authors sought to explore the identity work (Mendick 2006) of PSMTs analyzing how they use, and are used, by the discourses promoted within the course for positioning themselves as future mathematics teachers. The authors focused particularly on the discourse stating that "understanding mathematics in depth" is a necessary foundation for teaching the subject. In analyzing the contrasting experiences of two PSMTs, the authors showed that some PSMTs found it easier to take up the dominant discourse of "understanding mathematics in depth" for constructing themselves as mathematics teachers. But others resisted or distanced themselves of such discourse based on their cultural identities and backgrounds. This study highlighted the need to consider the various identities that PSMTs have prior to their participation in pre-service education and how these identities interact with the discourses promoted by pre-service education.

4 Discussion

The studies selected for this survey investigated different moments and opportunities that pre-service education offers to PSMTs for developing their professional identity. The notion of professional identity has been used as a theoretical lens for researching field experiences, technology use, the learning of mathematical topics, the curricular design of pre-service degree programs, the participation in communities, and the discourses promoted within pre-service courses. These varied research foci give rise to different conceptualizations of PSMTs identities; thus, the studies made use of varied theoretical terms such as "mathematical identity", "professional identity", "communal identity", or "identity work". Some articles also articulate the notion of subjectivity with the notion of identity (Brown et al. 2013; Hossain et al. 2013). These studies highlight the richness and the complexity of researching the identity development of PSMTs and underline the vital importance of researchers explaining how they read, understood, and operationalize professional identity in their works (Lerman 2012).

Regarding the theoretical perspectives underpinning the selected studies, the socio-cultural approaches were frequently used—they were used explicitly in four of the ten articles. However, it is important to acknowledge the emergence of post-structural and contemporary approaches for investigating the development of PSMTs' professional identities. We believe that those approaches can enable researchers to pose new questions regarding professional identities, illuminating new facets of the research problem.

Methodologically, the selected studies shared several features. With the exception of the theoretical paper of Bennison (2015) and the study of Gonçalves Costa and Pamplona (2011) centered in curriculum analysis, the rest of the studies were small-scale in-depth and qualitative. Thus, many of studies were case studies that varied in a number of one to ten PSMTs. This is consistent with the results of the survey on research methods used in mathematics teacher education carried out by Gellert et al. (2013) who found that small scale qualitative research predominates in the area. The data sources of the studies are varied: PSMTs' writings, semi-structured interviews, classroom observations, questionnaires, teachers' reflective writings, classroom audio-tapes and video recordings. The data collected were analyzed looking for emerging themes, using mainly an interpretative analysis. Lloyd's (2006) articles differed in this matter, since she developed a narrative analysis of the data. The selected studies differed in the way and the extent to which they explained the methods and techniques used for analyzing the data.

The results and findings of the studies were diverse and similar in nature. Most of them highlighted the importance of field experiences—mainly teaching practicum—during pre-service education as key settings for the development of PSMTs' professional identities. In resonance with other research results (Bergsten et al. 2009; Goos et al. 2009; Lin and Ponte 2009), the studies of Goos (2005), Goos and Bennison (2008), Van Putten et al. (2014), and Teixeira and Cyrino (2015) underline the teaching practicum as an experience where PSMTs enact their identities as mathematics teachers, navigating and negotiating between the constraints and affordances coming from the school and the university culture. Another finding shared by some of the studies (Bennison 2015; Brown et al. 2013; Gonçalves Costa and Pamplona 2011; Ticknor 2012), is that content courses are opportunities for PSMTs to develop self-understanding as mathematics apprentices. A particularly important issue emerging from the selected studies is that many of them explored the linkages between the PSMTs' identities as mathematics learners and PSMTs' professional future as teachers that will teach these topics to secondary students. Additionally, Lloyd's (2006) study highlighted the potential of narrative writing for expressing the ways in which PSMTs see themselves and for reflecting about their beliefs, values, and experiences. Finally, Hossain et al. (2013) drew attention to the discourses promoted within pre-service education, analyzing what they make possible for PSMTs to be and what they render impossible. Hossain et al.'s (2013) study enables us to reflect on our role as mathematics teacher educators in ensuring that all PSMTs have equitable access to becoming successful mathematics teachers.

5   Final Remarks

The studies selected for this survey suggest that investigating PSMTs professional identity development is an emergent topic in mathematics education research. They also pose some open questions that could be considered in upcoming research: the role of narrative writing as well as the roles of school teachers and university supervisors in the development of PSMTs professional identities; the linkages between identity development and agency development during teaching practicums; and the relationship between PSMTs' content knowledge and pedagogical content knowledge learned during pre-service education and the development of their professional identity.

This survey suggests several challenges in developing the professional identity of prospective teachers during pre-service education. Pre-service teacher education programs should offer time and space for PSMTs to reflect and discuss their knowledge and beliefs, as well as their views and expectations about becoming a mathematics teacher. In addition, pre-service teacher education programs should promote opportunities in which PSMTs reflect upon and interpret the social requisites and norms of their future teaching practices, as well as for acting upon different contexts in which these practices and discourses operate. This will help PSMT develop a sense of agency as they position themselves and gain autonomy "by taking into account their perspectives, knowledge and potentials" (Oliveira and Cyrino 2011, p. 114). It will also assist PSMTs in becoming aware of their political commitment as prospective educators and will contribute in forming responsible, autonomous and ethically demanding professionals, capable of effectively reflecting on their future pedagogical practice.

PSMTs' professional identities are rich and complex because they are produced in a rich and complex set of practices and discourses (Sachs 2005). Therefore, investigating PSMTs' identity development is a difficult enterprise. Nevertheless, this is an important enterprise because understanding PSMTs identities provides insights into why they make particular decisions (inside and outside the classroom) and into how mathematics teacher educators may assist them in developing their autonomy and agency.

Chapter 5
Current Research on Prospective Secondary Mathematics Teachers' Field Experiences

Marilyn E. Strutchens

1 Introduction

In recent years, more attention has been placed on field experiences of prospective teachers. In fact, a *Report of the Blue Ribbon Panel on Clinical Preparation and Partnerships for Improved Student Learning* commissioned by the National Council for Accreditation of Teacher Education [NCATE] (2010) in the U.S. suggests a "*clinically based preparation* for prospective teachers, which fully integrates content, pedagogy, and professional coursework around a core of clinical experiences" (p. 8). The clinical experiences suggested here would allow prospective teachers to learn to enact pedagogical strategies for particular purposes in context (Ball and Forzani 2009). In addition, NCATE (2010) suggests that prospective teachers experience a clinical experience continuum in which a developmental sequence of teaching experiences during the teacher education program is delineated with experiences moving from the simplest, such as learning names, recording grades, and taking the lunch count, to the most complex, such as differentiating instruction, developing assessments, and designing and implementing unit plans. These experiences would begin in a pre-teaching experience (mainly observational), next a practicum (perhaps teaching a lesson or working with small groups of students) connected to a methods course, and then finally an internship/student teaching experience (gradually taking on teaching responsibilities until he/she is teaching a full load of classes and then gradually gives the classes back to the cooperating teacher.).

Furthermore, the National Research Council [NRC] (2010) posited that field experience along with content knowledge and the quality of the prospective teachers are the aspects of teacher preparation that are likely to have the strongest

M.E. Strutchens (✉)
Auburn University, Auburn, AL, USA
e-mail: strutme@auburn.edu

© The Author(s) 2017
M.E. Strutchens et al., *The Mathematics Education of Prospective Secondary Teachers Around the World*, ICME-13 Topical Surveys,
DOI 10.1007/978-3-319-38965-3_5

effects on outcomes for students. In addition, teachers feel that clinical experiences are beneficial to their professional development:

> Study after study shows that experienced and newly certified teachers alike see clinical experiences (including student teaching) as a powerful—sometimes the single most powerful—component of teacher preparation. Whether that power enhances the quality of teacher preparation, however, may depend on the specific characteristics of the field experience. (Wilson et al. 2001, p. 17)

This implies that, during clinical experiences, prospective secondary mathematics teachers (PSMTs) develop *the craft of teaching*—the ability to design lessons that involve important mathematical ideas, design tasks that will help students to access those ideas, and to successfully carry out the lesson. This may include effectively launching the lesson, facilitating student engagement with the task, orchestrating meaningful mathematical discussions, and helping to make explicit the mathematical understanding students are constructing (Leatham and Peterson 2010, p. 115).

However, even though we would like prospective teachers to develop the craft of teaching as described, teacher preparation programs in many countries find it difficult to place PSMTs with cooperating teachers who are prepared to foster their growth due to many cooperating teachers' lack of proficiency with this approach to teaching, which is in alignment with the National Council of Teachers of Mathematics [NCTM] (1989, 1991, 1995, 2000, 2014) standards documents and other calls for inquiry-based and problem- and student-centered instruction. The cooperating teachers' lack of proficiency in using an inquiry approach to teaching may be attributed to their beliefs systems or lack of professional development related to the approach, or a combination of these factors and others.

Moreover, a bidirectional relationship needs to exist between teacher preparation programs and school partners in which clinical experiences take place. This relationship should reflect a common vision and shared commitment to inquiry-based practices and other issues related to mathematics teaching and learning. Borko et al. (2000) asserted that compatibility of methods courses and student teaching experiences in which PSMTs participate on several key dimensions is essential for the settings to reinforce each other's messages, and thus work in conjunction, rather than in opposition, to prepare reform-minded teachers.

Even though there have been calls for more attention to field experiences, there has not been many large scale studies that have looked at field experiences in a comprehensive manner. For example, the TEDs-M study only focused on whether or not programs within and across countries had *extended teaching practice* (student teaching) or *introductory field experiences* (pre-teaching or practicum) (Tatto et al. 2012). What follows is a review of the literature related to clinical experiences for PSMTs. The studies provided show the complexities that exist around clinical experiences and learning to teach in general.

2   Methodology of the Survey

The author conducted the survey by searching for studies related to field experiences for PSMTs published in nine international research journals in mathematics education (see Chap. 1 of the topic survey for a list of the journals). The search was confined to the relevant literature from the period of 2005–2015. Several searches were conducted by combining the key words "prospective teacher" and "secondary" with the following key words related to clinical experiences: "student teaching", "field placements", "mentor teachers" and "cooperating teachers". For each search result the article's title and abstract were read. The study was selected if it were connected to secondary prospective mathematics teachers' clinical experiences. Thus, the search excluded several studies that addressed field experiences of elementary prospective teachers. Next, the full articles were read and analyzed with regard to their (1) focus, (2) theoretical perspective, (3) methodology, and (4) findings. Then, the articles were categorized based on their research purposes. This analysis allowed me to divide the set of studies into 6 groups: (1) field experiences related to methods courses, (2) video-based explorations connected to methods courses, (3) a single case study related to student teaching, (4) articles that focused on the roles of PSMTs, cooperating teachers, and university supervisors, (5) professors reflecting on how to improve clinical experiences for their programs' candidates, and (6) programs' organization of field experience. I examined a total of 17 articles. Most of the studies examined in this topic study are qualitative in nature, which is not surprising due to the nature of field placements and the number of PSMTs that are usually in a program. Even though the majority of the studies may not be generalizable, they provide the field with detailed descriptions about the context and the participants involved in the studies, which can provide the field with information about promising practices and challenges.

3   The Selected Studies: What Has Been Studied in the Area?

3.1   Field Experiences Connected to Methods Courses

Four studies focused on field experiences connected to methods courses. Cavey and Berenson (2005) investigated a prospective teacher's understandings as she planned and exchanged ideas for teaching right triangle trigonometry in connection to concepts of ratio and proportion. They used Pirie–Kieren (1994) theory for growth in mathematical understanding as a lens for examining growth in the prospective teacher's understanding of mathematics within the context of learning to teach mathematics (as cited in Cavey and Berenson 2005). The researchers found that significant growth in understanding can occur when PSMTs have multiple opportunities to share and reflect on their images of teaching mathematics.

Nguyen et al. (2008) examined a case study of three Vietnamese student teachers working in groups in a methods course to explore Freudenthal's theory of realistic mathematics education (RME). The course emphasized students' knowledge construction in meaningful contexts. Qualitative methods were utilized. Transcripts of class discussions and group discussions, interviews, student teachers' lesson plans, and journal writings were the main data sources that were used to investigate the development of the student teachers' views on mathematics and mathematics education during the course. The deliberations about teaching strategies of the three subjects working in a group to design lesson plans were also analyzed. The findings showed that the three student teachers explored new meanings of mathematics teaching that caused them to shift from their traditional point of view to a student-centered one. Reflecting on their teaching and learning also impacted their decision to utilize the student-centered approach. It is noted that among the three subjects, there were two student teachers, who questioned the viability of the student-centered approach in the Vietnamese educational context where the social and political conditions were not favorable for teaching in this manner.

Ricks (2011) discussed a theoretical framework that divides teacher reflection into two broad categories: "The first and most common incident reflection occurs as specific incidents or episodes unconnected to future activity. The second process reflection—based on the work of John Dewey and Donald Schön—connects reflective incidents into a cyclic progression that refines ideas through experimental action" (p. 251). He examined the reflective activity of a group of prospective secondary mathematics teachers as they jointly planned a public school lesson to illustrate how incidents of reflection can be refined and linked into more powerful and purposeful progressions of ideas.

These studies provide evidence that it is important for PSMTs to connect what they are doing in their course work to what is happening in classrooms. The studies also helped reinforce the need for field experiences to be embedded throughout PSMTs' programs.

3.2   Using Video-Cases to Foster PSMTs Understanding of NCTM's Standards Based and Inquiry-Based Approaches

Studies in this section used videos as a means to help PSMTs understand what reform based teaching looks like, serving as a "virtual" field experience. This approach aids with the dilemma discussed in the introduction related to the number of secondary mathematics teachers who are strong reform mathematics teachers. Santagata et al. (2007) reported on two studies in which a video-based program on lesson analysis for pre-service mathematics teachers was implemented for two consecutive years as part of a teacher education program at the University of Lazio, Italy. The authors gave a rationale for using video cases to help PSMTs analyze teaching and learning situations. They addressed two questions: What can prospective teachers learn from the analysis of videotaped lessons? How can prospective teachers' analysis ability, and its improvement, be measured? Two groups of prospective teachers (approximately 140 in total) participated in the program. A three-step lesson analysis framework was applied to three lesson videos: (1) goal(s) and parts of the lesson; (2) student learning; and, (3) teaching alternatives. Prospective teachers' ability to analyze lessons was measured through an open-ended pre- and post-assessment. In the assessment, prospective teachers were asked to mark and comment on events (in a lesson not included in the program) that they found interesting for: teachers' actions/decisions; students' behavior/learning; and, mathematical content. A coding system was developed based on five criteria: elaboration, mathematics content, student learning, critical approach, and alternative strategies. The researchers found that in a relatively short period of time, prospective teachers in both Study 1 and Study 2 improved their analyses of teaching by moving from simple descriptions of what they observed to analyses focused on the effects of teacher actions on student learning as observed in the video. These data suggest promising directions for the development of both an instrument to measure lesson analysis abilities and a model for teacher learning.

In addition, Stockero (2008) employed mixed methods to investigate the effects of using a coherent video-case curriculum in a university mathematics methods course to determine: (1) how the use of a video-case curriculum affects the reflective stance of PSMTs; and (2) the extent to which a reflective stance developed while reflecting on other teachers' practice transfers to reflecting on one's own practice. 21 third-year PSMTs who were enrolled in a middle school (grades 6–8) mathematics methods course participated in the study. Stockero (2008) cited and Sherins' (2008) and Manouchehri's (2002) studies, which focus on levels of reflection as the basis for her theoretical framework. According to Stockero (2008), a key component of the course was a field experience with an intensive reflection component, which consisted of three visits to local middle school mathematics classrooms immediately following the completion of the video-case curriculum. The PSMTs all visited one or two classrooms at the same time; each PSMT facilitated a small group of students as they worked to solve a mathematics problem that was taken directly from the video-case materials. Stockero (2008) found that the PSMTs in the study showed changes in their level of reflection, their tendency to ground their analyses in evidence, and their focus on student thinking. She asserted that they began to analyze how teaching affects student thinking, to consider multiple interpretations of student thinking, and to develop a more tentative stance of inquiry. She also stated that the reflective stance developed via the video curriculum transferred to the PSMTs' self-reflection in the course's field experience.

Alsawaie and Alghazo (2010) used an experimental design, which involved mathematics PSMTs in analyzing video-based lessons and tested the effect of this experience on the PSMTs' ability to analyze mathematics teaching. They cited the learning to notice framework developed by van Es and Sherin (2002) and elaborated on in van Es and Sherin (2008) as their theoretical underpinning. Twenty-six

PSMTs who were enrolled in a mathematics methods course participated in the study. Half were in a control group. The students in the experimental group watched the videos on their own time at home. The authors believe that the intervention described in the study helped the PSMTs learn to pay attention to noteworthy events in classroom interactions; also, they developed the ability to pay attention to student learning when watching and analyzing a lesson.

Two of the studies in this session used similar theoretical frameworks related to reflecting on practice. All three of the studies showed that video-based instruction can be helpful in increasing PSMTs ability to analyze teaching and learning situations with a focus on learning.

3.3   Single Case Study Related to the Student Teaching Experience

Lloyd (2005) presented a case study of a PSMT, which focused on the teacher's beliefs about his role as mathematics teacher. Data were collected over the final 5 months of the teacher's university teacher education program through interviews, written course assignments, and observations of student-teaching. Findings indicated that the prospective teacher valued classroom roles in which students, rather than the teacher, explained traditional mathematics content. As his student-teaching internship progressed, the teacher began to develop new roles and engaged students in additional mathematical processes. These results emphasize the need for prospective teachers to recognize how teacher and student roles impact interrelationships between understanding and mathematical activity, and illustrate the nature of teacher learning that can occur during an internship. Lloyd (2005) suggested that activities that require the PSMTs to critically examine the roles of teacher and students, and related development of mathematics, in diverse representations of classroom instruction such as videotaped lessons or written classroom cases may move them in this direction.

3.4   Studies Related to the Roles of PSMTs, Cooperating Teachers, and University Supervisors During the Student Teaching Experience

These studies show the importance of placing student teachers in classrooms with teachers' whose practices are in alignment with program goals and who understand that the student teaching experience should be one of growth mathematically for all stakeholders including the PSMT, cooperating teacher, students, and the university supervisor.

Peterson and Williams (2008) shared two contrasting case studies of student teachers and their cooperating teachers that illustrated very different experiences with mathematical knowledge during student teaching. The researchers cited the work of Ball et al. (2005) as the framework for the knowledge that PSMTs need for teaching. The data for this study is taken from a study of eight student teacher/cooperating teacher pairs, and the core themes that emerged from their conversations. Peterson and Williams (2008) focused on two pairs for whom the core conversational themes represented disparate approaches to mathematics in and for teaching. One pair, Blake and Mr. B., focused on controlling student behavior and rarely talked about mathematics for teaching. The other pair, Tara and Mr. T., focused on having students actively participating in the lesson and on mathematics from the students' point of view. These contrasting experiences suggested that student teaching can have a profound effect on prospective teachers' understanding of mathematics in and for teaching. One finding from the study highlighted by the authors was "the consonance between the cooperating teachers' stated beliefs about mathematics teaching and what they wanted student teachers to learn, their mentoring style, and the focus of conversations with student teachers" (Peterson and Williams 2008, p. 475.).

Fernandez and Erbilgin (2009) conducted a qualitative study of post-lesson conferences led by supervisors (classroom cooperating teachers and a university supervisor) working with mathematics student teachers. They examined the issue through a sociocultural lens. They found that cooperating teachers focused more on evaluative supervision that lacked attention to the mathematics of the lessons, while the university supervisor focused more on educative supervision, guiding student teachers to reflect on and learn from their own classroom experiences including the mathematics of their lessons.

Leatham and Peterson (2010) reported on the results of a survey of 45 secondary mathematics cooperating teachers' perceptions of the primary purposes of student teaching and their roles in accomplishing those purposes. The three most common categories (teacher interaction, real classroom, and classroom management) made up more than 70 % of the total number of responses. Based on their results, the researchers asserted that for the cooperating teachers who mentor their PSMTs, the primary purpose of student teaching is to interact with experienced teachers in real classrooms, and in so doing to learn how to successfully manage such classrooms. They concluded that in order for the student teaching experience to meet the needs of PSMTs to learn how to teach mathematics in meaningful ways so that student learning may occur, it would be helpful (i) to articulate the most important purposes of student teaching and then (ii) to define the roles that teacher educators, cooperating teachers, and PSMTs need to play to accomplish those purposes.

Rhoads et al. (2010) explored prospective secondary mathematics teachers' "professed philosophies of teaching" and how they felt they compared to those of their cooperating teachers. They further explored the prospective teachers' views of important factors impacting relationships with mentors, including cooperating teachers and university mentors. The subjects of the study were graduates of a post-baccalaureate teacher certification program at a large state university in the U.S.; while graduates are certified to teach mathematics grades K-12, most elect to teach high school. Semi-structured interviews, lasting 1–2 h, were held with 9 subjects. A constant-comparative method was used to analyze the transcripts. While most of the student teachers spoke against an overemphasis on procedures, all of them worked with at least one cooperating teacher who they felt emphasized procedures; four of the nine felt this mismatch negatively impacted their experience. Four of the student teachers had positive relationships with their cooperating teachers; factors impacting their relationship included honest and constructive feedback, a sense of "kinship," and freedom in their teaching. Negative factors impacting the relationship included inadequate feedback and difficult personal relationships. "Candid and relevant" feedback and emotional support were important factors for positive relationships with the university supervisor (Rhoads et al. 2010, p. 1016); inadequate feedback was an important factor in negative relationships. A lack of content knowledge by the supervisor was also cited as a negative factor. The authors note that these results are limited in that they rely only on reports of the student teachers; gaining other perspectives would provide valuable insights.

Rhoads et al. (2013) investigated interpersonal difficulties that student teachers and cooperating teachers may experience during the teaching internship by exploring the tension between one high school mathematics student teacher and his cooperating teacher. The data came from multiple sources, including individual interviews with Luis, the student teacher, and Sheri, his cooperating teacher, about their internship experiences; the evaluations of Luis's teaching that were provided separately by Sheri, the university supervisor, and a second cooperating teacher; 20 pages of hand-written notes that Sheri provided for Luis during the beginning part of his student teaching experience; and an interview with the university supervisor. The authors identified seven causes of the tension that existed between Luis and Sheri, which included different ideas about what mathematics should be taught, how it should be taught, and a strained personal relationship. The researchers compared these findings with results from interviews with six other student teachers and eight of their mentors to explore the uniqueness of this case. As a result of the study, Rhoads et al. (2013) posited that it is important for PSMTs and cooperative teachers to discuss common issues that can arise during the internship and ways to communicate openly about philosophies of teaching and philosophies of mentoring. They also suggested that cooperating teachers and PSMTs be encouraged to approach the internship with mutual respect, open minds, and a willingness to learn from their colleagues.

3.5   Professors Reflecting on How to Improve Clinical Experiences for Their Prospective Teachers

Goodell (2006) reported the results of a 4-year naturalistic study, which focused on how her students learned to become mathematics teachers during the combined 15-week methods and field placement course that she teaches. She determined the critical incidents that PSMTs encountered during their field experience and what they learned about teaching for understanding through reflecting on those critical incidents. The researcher noted that PSMTs raised issues in their incident reports that focused on four main areas: teaching and classroom management; student factors such as pre-requisite knowledge, understanding, resistance and motivation; issues concerning relationships with colleagues, students and parents; and school organizational issues such as policies and access to resources. She also found that the PSMTs' learning about teaching for understanding focused on three broad areas: the conditions necessary to teach for understanding; facilitation of teaching for understanding; and barriers to teaching for understanding. One of the major recommendations provided by Goodell (2006) as a result of her analysis is "teacher education programs that are serious about developing teachers' abilities to become reflective practitioners must make a commitment to assigning full-time faculty to field experiences, and to linking those experiences to methods classes" (p. 242).

Nolan (2012) described how she transformed and reformed her own practice as a teacher educator and faculty advisor by listening to the stories of prospective teachers. Data for the study included interviews and focus groups with eight interns with whom she worked during two internship semesters. The intent of her interviews was to understand how interns reflected on their own processes of learning to teach and of negotiating spaces for agency during their field experience. Nolan (2012) used Bourdieu's social field theory, which highlights the network of relations and discursive practices that support (and (re)produce) traditional practices in the teaching of mathematics the theoretical underpinning for her study.

3.6   Program Organization of Field Experiences

In response to the Third International Mathematics and Science Study (TIMSS) video study, which showed clear differences in how teachers from the U.S. and Japan teach, Peterson (2005) explored why this is the case by comparing the preparation of Japanese to that of U.S. prospective teachers. Based on field notes collected during observations of student teachers at three Japanese universities for 3 or 4 days each, he described the general student teaching experience in comparison to that in the U.S. Differences were found in the school context and the structure of lessons, which tended to focused on having students engage in problem solving. The duration and organization of the student teaching experience were also different, with students teaching for 2–3 week periods in several contexts; in addition, they were typically assigned to cooperating teachers in groups. The focus of the student teaching experience is also quite different, with primary attention given to preparing, teaching, and reflecting on selected lessons. The cooperating teacher and group of student teachers assigned to him/her provided intensive feedback on each lesson plan to be taught by a student teacher prior to it being taught, observed their teaching of the lesson, and participated in a reflection meeting after the lesson. Throughout this process, focus was placed on the structure of the lesson and its impact on student thinking, rather than the presentation of the lesson. Peterson (2005) concluded that this emphasis on lesson preparation might be useful for U.S. teacher educators to consider.

Arbaugh et al. (2007) explored viewpoints surrounding field experiences in a post-baccalaureate certification program for secondary mathematics and science teachers. Such programs can be completed in a short period of time following completion of an undergraduate degree, which raises questions about how to incorporate effective field experiences. The program the authors designed and studied was grounded in Shulman's work on pedagogical content knowledge (PCK) and how to create a "transformative pathway" (Arbaugh et al. 2007, p. 193), which led them to create a year-long internship experience. They collected data during a day-long meeting of students, cooperating teachers, and university personnel in which participants evaluated different ways of organizing the field experience—such as participating every day but perhaps for less than a full day versus participating full days but perhaps not every day, and one single year-long placement versus multiple shorter placements. They also conducted exit interviews at the end of the year. Arbaugh et al. (2007) found that while all three groups liked the intensity of the year-long model, they had very different ideas about how the experience should be organized, based on their personal needs and experiences. The interns preferred the every-day model in which they participated half-days, which was similar to what they were experiencing. They felt this provided more depth in seeing how content developed as well as more flexibility in scheduling. In contrast, the coopering teachers had more reservations about the students only teaching half-days, noting that is does not reflect the full teacher role and creates more disruptions. The university personnel saw merits in the half-day format, since its flexibility might help with recruitment, but felt that two semester-long placements might be more effective given difficulties in identifying year-long placements. The authors used these findings to adapt their model for the next cohort so that it would better meet the needs of the different stakeholders in alignment with their emphasis on PCK and creating transformative pathways.

4 Discussion

The studies included in this survey focused on different aspects of the field experiences provided to PSMTs—field experiences connected to methods courses, use of video cases as "virtual" field experiences, and summative student teaching experiences. Studies focusing on the student teaching experience addressed the roles of those involved in the experience, how the experience is organized, and how it can be improved. These studies provide useful insights into effective incorporation of field experiences into the preparation of PSMTs.

Interestingly, very few of these studies took an explicit theoretical stance, instead framing their research within more specific frameworks specific to the question being addressed, such as realistic mathematics education (Nguyen et al. 2008), teacher reflection (Ricks 2011) or learning to notice (Alawaise and Alghazo 2010). In general, the studies tended to focus on more pragmatic concerns related to providing effective field experiences and were less focused on theory building.

Nearly all of the studies used qualitative methods with relatively small numbers of subjects. This is perhaps not surprising due to the nature of field placements and the small number of PSMTs that are typically engaged in a field experience. Case studies were commonly employed, but with different subjects, including a single or small group of PSMT (Cavey and Berenson 2005; Lloyd 2005; Nguyen et al. 2008), student teachers and their mentors (Fernandez and Erbilgin 2009; Peterson and Williams 2008; Rhoads et al. 2013), or themselves (Goodell 2006; Nolan 2012). Of studies using quantitative methods, all focused on PSMT during field experiences associated with methods classes (Alsawaie and Alghazo 2010; Leatham and Peterson 2010; Santagata et al. 2007; Stockeroo 2008); all but one had a sample size less than 50.

Even though the designs and sample size may limit the generalizability of results, these studies provide the field with detailed descriptions about the context and the participants involved in the studies, which can provide the field with information about promising practices and challenges. It is important that PSMTs have coursework that is integrated with field experiences to promote reflection on what it means to teach mathematics (Cavey and Berenson 2005; Nguyen et al. 2008; Ricks 2011). Video cases can serve as a "virtual" field experience to help PSMTs understand what reform-based teaching looks like (Santagata et al. 2007; Stockeroo 2008). Other studies suggest the importance of understanding the roles of PSMTs, their cooperating teacher, and their university supervisors within the student teaching experience and the difficulties that may arise (Fernadez and Erbilgin 2009; Leatham and Peterson 2010; Rhoads et al. 2010, 2012). Teacher educators might also interrogate how student teaching experiences are organized (Arbaugh et al. 2007; Peterson 2005) and actively reflect on their own practice (Goodell 2006; Nolan 2012).

In conclusion, it is somewhat surprising that this survey uncovered so few studies that carefully research the field experiences of PSMTs, given the importance of those experiences within teacher preparation programs. Preparing PSMTs seems to be an area ripe for new researchers to explore, building on a number of careful studies presented in this section that suggest useful areas for exploration.

Chapter 6
Summary and Looking Ahead

Marilyn E. Strutchens, Rongjin Huang, Leticia Losano,
Despina Potari, João Pedro da Ponte, Márcia Cristina de
Costa Trindade Cyrino and Rose Mary Zbiek

Throughout the survey one can see that there is a steady growth in the research around prospective secondary mathematics teacher education. Also several of the studies were repeated in at least two of the sections due to the nature of the factors that were studied. It is difficult to write about teacher knowledge without some acknowledgment of how knowledge or lack of knowledge can impact teachers' mathematics identities. Furthermore, field experiences are contexts in which PSMTs' knowledge and identities are impacted and shaped. In addition, the survey revealed that mathematics education researchers are thinking more deeply about how to foster the growth of effective mathematics teachers in a myriad of ways.

For example, we know more about teacher education strategies that appear to have a positive impact on the development of PSMT knowledge, such as designing classroom tasks, looking closer at students' thinking, and linking theoretical models

M.E. Strutchens (✉)
Department of Curriculum and Teaching, Auburn University, Auburn, AL, USA

R. Huang
Department of Mathematical Sciences, Middle Tennessee State University, Murfreesboro, TN, USA

L. Losano
Facultad de Matemática, Universidad Nacional de Córdoba, Córdoba, Córdoba, Argentina

D. Potari
Mathematics Department Panepistimiouloli, National and Kapodistrian University of Athens, Athens, Greece

J.P. da Ponte
Instituto de Educação, Universidade de Lisboa, Lisbon, Portugal

M.C. de C.T. Cyrino
Department of Mathematics, State University of Londrina, Londrina, Brazil

R.M. Zbiek
College of Education, The Pennsylvania State University, University Park, PA, USA

© The Author(s) 2017   45
M.E. Strutchens et al., *The Mathematics Education of Prospective
Secondary Teachers Around the World*, ICME-13 Topical Surveys,
DOI 10.1007/978-3-319-38965-3_6

to teaching and learning phenomena. Initial attempts have also been made to study the actual interaction in teacher education contexts and in close relation to PSMT field experiences. However, more efforts need to be made to extend our teacher education practices in directions that address the complexity of mathematics teaching and to see teacher knowledge in the broader context of building teaching identities.

Moreover, limited literature suggests that incorporating appropriate technologies in teacher preparation programs could help PSMTs deepen understanding of content knowledge and pedagogical knowledge, and develop positive dispositions for using technology. Consistent use of technology in content and methods courses, and field experiences could help PSMTs develop an awareness of implementing reform-oriented instruction. However, much remains unknown about how to develop and implement materials and initiatives to help PSMTs develop and employ the forms of knowledge found in the TPACK framework. Systematic redesign of courses, the connection between course design, and teaching practicum need to be explored on a large scale. Thus, preparing PSMTs to teach secondary mathematics with technology is an important endeavor and an emerging research area in need of systematic studies and a global effort to develop a cohesive body of literature.

In addition, some key findings were presented related to the emergence of PSMTs professional identities. PSMTs' professional identities are largely shaped by their field experiences and content courses. Therefore, it is important to explore the linkages between the PSMTs' identities as mathematics learners and PSMTs professional future as teachers who will teach mathematical topics to secondary students. Asking PSMTs to write personal narratives is an important strategy utilized by mathematics teacher educators to learn more about the beliefs, values, and experiences of PSMTs, Conducting the survey made it evident that the development of PSMTs identities is an emergent research topic that provides important insights into why PSMTs make particular decisions (inside and outside the classroom) and into how mathematics teacher educators may assist them in developing their autonomy and agency.

The survey of the field experience literature revealed that much of the work is at a small scale and that much of the work has not been replicated in other places. While these studies provide useful beginning points for better understanding the field experiences provided to PSMTs, there seems to be little concern for carefully building theory around field experiences. The lack of common framing across the studies increases the difficulty of building more general understanding of the purpose, place, and effective use of field experiences. Despite the inherent difficulties in building larger sample sizes, attempting to do so by building on some of the promising findings from these studies seems like a worthwhile endeavor. For example, a collaboration of researchers across multiple programs may be able to create a sufficient sample size to undertake larger-scale investigations. Alternatively, phenomena might be tracked over a longer period of time with the same set of subjects in order to create more robust data sets.

As stated earlier the study of PSMTs needs to continue to grow, and more of the work needs to be published in major mathematics education journals. Links between PSMTs' knowledge, identity, use of technology, and field experiences are needed in order to capture the complexity of the process of becoming a mathematics teacher. Large scale and longitudinal studies are also needed to help us to understand the effectiveness of secondary mathematics teacher preparation programs.

References

Adler, J., & Davis, Z. (2006). Opening another black box: Researching mathematics for teaching in mathematics teacher education. *Journal for Research in Mathematics Education, 37*, 270–296.

Adler, J., Hossain, S., Stevenson, M., Clarke, J., Archer, R., & Grantham, B. (2014). Mathematics for teaching and deep subject knowledge: Voices of mathematics enhancement course students in England. *Journal of Mathematics Teacher Education, 17*, 129–148.

Aguirre, J. M., Zaval, M. R., & Katanoutanant, T. (2012). Developing robust forms of pre-service teachers' pedagogical content knowledge through culturally responsive mathematics teaching analysis. *Mathematics Teacher Education and Development, 14*, 113–136.

Akkoç, H. (2015). Formative questioning in computer learning environments: A course for pre-service mathematics teachers. *International Journal of Mathematical Education in Science and Technology, 46*, 1096–1115.

Alajmi, A. H. (2015). Algebraic generalization strategies used by Kuwaiti pre-service teachers. *International Journal of Science and Mathematics Education*, (online first). doi:10.1007/s10763-015-9657-y.

Alsawaie, O. N., & Alghazo, I. M. (2010). The effect of video-based approach of prospective teachers' ability to analyze mathematics teaching. *Journal of Mathematics Teacher Education, 13*, 232–241.

Arbaugh, F., Abell, S., Lannin, J., Volkmann, M., & Boone, W. (2007). Field-Based internship models for alternative certification of science and mathematics teachers: Views of interns, mentors, and university educators. *Eurasia Journal of Mathematics, Science & Technology Education, 3*(3), 191–201.

Ball, D., & Bass, H. (2000). Interweaving content and pedagogy in teaching and learning to teach: Knowing and using mathematics. In J. Boaler (Ed.), *Multiple perspectives on mathematics teaching and learning* (pp. 83–104). Westport, CT: Ablex Publishing.

Ball, D., Thames, M. H., & Phelps, G. (2008). Content knowledge for teaching: What makes it special? *Journal of Teacher Education, 59*, 389–407.

Ball, D. L., & Forzani, F. M. (2009). The work of teaching and the challenge for teacher education. *Journal of Teacher Education, 60*, 497–511.

Baumert, J., Kunter, M., Blum, W., Brunner, M., Voss, T., Jordan, A., et al. (2010). Teachers' mathematical knowledge, cognitive activation in the classroom, and student progress. *American Educational Research Journal, 47*(1), 133–180.

Beijaard, D., Verloop, N., & Vermunt, J. D. (2000). Teachers' perceptions of professional identity: An exploratory study from a personal knowledge perspective. *Teaching and Teacher Education, 16*, 749–764.

Bennison, A. (2015). Developing an analytic lens for investigating identity as an embedder-of-numeracy. *Mathematics Education Research Journal, 27*(1), 1–19.

© The Author(s) 2017
M.E. Strutchens et al., *The Mathematics Education of Prospective Secondary Teachers Around the World*, ICME-13 Topical Surveys,
DOI 10.1007/978-3-319-38965-3

Bergsten, C., Barbro, G., & Franco, F. (2009). Learning to teach mathematics: Expanding the role of practicum as an integrated part of a teacher education programme. In R. Even & D. Ball (Eds.), *The professional education and development of teachers of mathematics. The 15th ICMI Study* (pp. 57–70). New York: Springer.

Bernstein, B. (1996). *Pedagogy, symbolic control and identity: Theory, research, critique.* London: Taylor & Francis.

Black, L., Mendick, H., & Solomon, Y. (2009). *Mathematical relationships in education: Identities and participation.* New York: Routledge.

Blömeke, S., & Delaney, S. (2012). Assessment of teacher knowledge across countries: A review of the state of research. *ZDM Mathematics Education, 44*, 223–247.

Blömeke, S., Hsieh, F. J., Kaiser, G., & Schmidt, W. (2014). *International perspectives on teacher knowledge, beliefs and opportunities to learn.* Dordrecht: Springer.

Borko, H., Peressini, D., Romagnano, L., Knuth, E., & Willis, C. (2004). A conceptual framework for learning to teach secondary mathematics: A situative perspective. *Educational Studies in Mathematics, 56*, 67–96.

Borko, H., Virmani, R., Khachatryan, E., & Mangram, C. (2014). The roles of video-based discussions in professional development and the preparation of professional development leaders. In B. D. Calandra & P. Rich (Eds.), *Digital video for teacher education: Research and practice* (pp. 89–108). Philadelphia, RA: Routledge.

Boylan, M. (2010). It's getting me thinking and I'm an old cynic: Exploring the relational dynamics of mathematics teacher change. *Journal of Mathematics Teacher Education, 13*, 383–395.

Brown, T., & McNamara, O. (2011). *Becoming a mathematics teacher: Identity and Identifications.* New York: Springer.

Brown, T., Heywood, D., Solomon, Y., & Zagorianakos, A. (2013). Experiencing the space we share: Rethinking subjectivity and objectivity. *ZDM Mathematics Education, 45*, 561–572.

Caglayan, G. (2013). Prospective mathematics teachers' sense making of polynomial multiplication and factorization modeled with algebra tiles. *Journal of Mathematics Teacher Education, 16*, 349–378.

Capraro, M. M., An, S. A., Ma, T., Rangel-Chavez, A. F., & Harbaugh, A. (2012). An investigation of preservice teachers' use of guess and check in solving a semi open-ended mathematics problem. *Journal of Mathematical Behavior, 31*, 105–116.

Capraro, M. M., Capraro, R. M., & Helfeldt, J. (2010). Do differing types of field experiences make a difference in teacher candidates' perceived level of competence? *Teacher Education Quarterly, 37*(1), 131–154.

Carrejo, D. J., & Marshall, J. (2007). What is mathematical modelling? Exploring prospective teachers' use of experiments to connect mathematics to the study of motion. *Mathematics Education Research Journal, 19*, 45–76.

Cavey, L. O., & Berenson, S. B. (2005). Learning to teach high school mathematics: Patterns of growth in understanding right triangle trigonometry during lesson plan study. *Journal of Mathematical Behavior, 24*, 171–190.

Charalambous, Ch. (2015). Working at the intersection of teacher knowledge, teacher beliefs, and teaching practice: A multiple-case study. *Journal of Mathematics Teacher education, 18*, 427–445.

Clark, K. M. (2012). History of mathematics: Illuminating understanding of school mathematics concepts for prospective mathematics teachers. *Educational Studies in Mathematics, 81*, 67–84.

Clarke, P. J. (2009). A Caribbean pre-service mathematics teacher's impetus to integrate computer technology in his practice. *International Journal for Technology in Mathematics Education, 16*(4), 145–154.

Cochran-Smith, M., & Villegas, A. M. (2015). Studying teacher preparation: The questions that drive research. *European Educational Research Journal, 14*(5), 1–16.

Corleis, A., Schwarz, B., Kaiser, G., & Leung, I. K. C. (2008). Content and pedagogical content knowledge in argumentation and proof of future teachers: A comparative case study in Germany and Hong Kong. *ZDM Mathematics Education, 44*, 223–247.

Cory, B. L., & Garofalo, J. (2011). Using dynamic sketches to enhance pre-service secondary mathematics teachers' understanding of limits of sequences. *Journal for Research in Mathematics Education, 42*, 65–97.

Daher, W. M., & Shahbari, J. A. (2015). Pre-service teachers' modeling processes through engagement with model eliciting activities with a technological tool. *International Journal of Science and Mathematics Education, 13*, 25–46.

Davis, J. D. (2009). Understanding the influence of two mathematics textbooks on prospective secondary teachers' knowledge. *Journal of Mathematics Teacher Education, 12*, 365–389.

Davis, J. D. (2015). Prospective mathematics teachers' interactions with CAS-based textbook elements. *International Journal for Technology in Mathematics Education, 22*(3), 107–113.

Day, C., Elliot, B., & Kington, A. (2005). Reform, standards and teacher identity: Challenges of sustaining commitment. *Teaching and Teacher Education, 21*(5), 563–577.

Delice, A., & Kertil, M. (2015). Investigating the representational fluency of preservice mathematics teachers in a modeling process. *International Journal of Science and Mathematics Education* (online first).

Demircioglu, H., Argun, Z., & Bulut, S. (2010). A case study: Assessment of preservice secondary mathematics teachers' metacognitive behavior in the problem-solving process. *ZDM Mathematics Education, 42*, 493–502.

Döhrmann, M., Kaiser, G., & Blömeke, S. (2012). The conceptualisation of mathematics competencies in the international teacher education study TEDS-M. *ZDM Mathematics Education, 44*, 325–340.

Eli, J. A., Mohr-Schroeder, M. J., & Lee, C. W. (2011). Exploring mathematical connections of prospective middle-grades teachers through card-sorting tasks. *Mathematics Education Research Journal, 23*, 297–319.

Fernandez, M. L., & Erbilgin, E. (2009). Examining the supervision of mathematics student teachers through analysis of conference communications. *Educational Studies in Mathematics, 72*, 93–110.

Fraser, W., Garofalo, J., & Juersivich, N. (2011). Enhancing lesson planning and quality of classroom life: A study of mathematics student teachers' use of technology. *Journal of Technology and Teacher Education, 19*(2), 169–188.

Gama, R., & Fiorentini, D. (2008). Identidade de professores iniciantes de matemática que participam de grupos colaborativos. *Horizontes (EDUSF), 26*, 31–43. [In Frience]

Gellert, U., Becerra, R., & Chapman, O. (2013). Research methods in mathematics teacher education. In M. A. Clements, A. J. Bishop, C. Keitel, J. Kilpatrick, & F. K. S. Leung (Eds.), *Third international handbook of mathematics education* (pp. 327–360). New York: Springer.

Gonçalves, M. A., & De Carvalho, D. L. (2014). Perscrutando diários de aulas e produzindo narrativas sobre a disciplina estágio supervisionado de um curso de licenciatura em matemática. *Bolema, 28*(49), 777–798.

Gonçalves Costa, W. N., & Pamplona, A. S. (2011). Entrecruzando fronteiras: A educação estatística na formação de professores de matemática. *Bolema, 24*(40), 897–911.

Goodell, J. (2006). Using critical incident reflections: A self-study as a mathematics teacher educator. *Journal of Mathematics Teacher Education, 9*, 221–248.

Goos, M. (2005). A sociocultural analysis of the development of pre-service and beginning teachers' pedagogical identities as users of technology. *Journal of Mathematics Teacher Education, 8*, 35–59.

Goos, M., & Bennison, A. (2008). Developing a communal identity as beginning teachers of mathematics: Emergence of an online community of practice. *Journal of Mathematics Teacher Education, 11*, 41–60.

Goos, M., Arvold, B., Bednarz, N., DeBlois, L., Maheux, J., Morselli, F., et al. (2009). School experience during pre-service teacher education from the students' perspective. In R. Even & D. L. Ball (Eds.), *The professional education and development of teachers of mathematics* (pp. 83–91). New York: Springer.

Graven, M., & Lerman, S. (2014). Mathematics teacher identity. In S. Lerman (Ed.), *Encyclopedia of mathematics education* (pp. 434–438). Dordrecht: Springer.

Groth, R. E., & Bergner, J. A. (2013). Mapping the structure of knowledge for teaching nominal categorical data analysis. *Educational Studies in Mathematics, 83,* 247–265.

Haciomeroglu, E. S., Bu, L., Schoen, R. C., & Hohenwarter, M. (2010). Prospective teachers' experiences in developing lessons with dynamic mathematics software. *International Journal for Technology in Mathematics Education, 18*(2), 71–82.

Hähkiöniemi, M., & Leppäaho, H. (2011). Prospective mathematics teachers' ways of Guiding high school students in GeoGebra-supported inquiry tasks. *International Journal for Technology in Mathematics Education, 19*(2), 45–57.

Halat, E. (2011). Perspectives of pre-service middle and secondary mathematics teachers on the use of Webquests in teaching and learning geometry. *International Journal for Technology in Mathematics Education, 16*(1), 27–36.

Hannigan, A., Gill, O., & Leavy, A. M. (2013). An investigation of prospective secondary mathematics teachers' conceptual knowledge of and attitudes towards statistics. *Journal of Mathematics Teacher Education, 16,* 427–449.

Hossin, S., Mendrick, H., & Adler, J. (2013). Troubling "understanding mathematics in-depth": Its role in the identity work of student-teachers in England. *Educational Studies in Mathematics, 84,* 32–48.

Huang, R., & Kulm, G. (2012). Prospective middle grade mathematics teachers' knowledge of algebra for teaching. *Journal of Mathematical Behavior, 31,* 417–430.

Jenkins, O. F. (2010). Developing teachers' knowledge of students as learners of mathematics through structured interviews. *Journal of Mathematics Teacher Education, 13,* 141–154.

Johnson, H. L., Blume, G. W., Shimizu, J. K., Graysay, D., & Konnova, S. (2014). A teacher's conception of definition and use of examples when doing and teaching mathematics. *Mathematical Thinking and Learning, 16,* 285–311.

Kaarstein, H. (2015). *Modeling, operationalising and measuring mathematics pedagogical content knowledge: Threats to construct validity* (Ph.D. dissertation, University of Oslo, Norway).

Karp, A. (2010). Analyzing and attempting to overcome prospective teachers' difficulties during problem-solving instruction. *Journal of Mathematics Teacher Education, 13,* 121–139.

Kelchtermans, G. (2009). Who I am in how I teach is the message: Self-understanding, vulnerability and reflection. *Teachers and Teaching, 15*(2), 257–272.

Koehler, M. J., & Mishra, P. (2008). Introducing technological pedagogical content knowledge. In AACTE Committee on Innovation and Technology (Eds.), *Handbook of technological pedagogical content knowledge (TPCK) for educators* (pp. 3–29). New York: Routledge.

Koirala, H. P., Davis, M., & Johnson, P. (2008). Development of a performance assessment task and rubric to measure prospective secondary school mathematics teachers' pedagogical content knowledge. *Journal of Mathematics Teacher Education, 11,* 127–138.

Koparan, T. (2016). The effect on prospective teachers of the learning environment supported by dynamic statistics software. *International Journal of Mathematical Education in Science and Technology, 47,* 276–290.

Krauss, S., Baumert, J., & Blum, W. (2008). Secondary mathematics teachers' pedagogical content knowledge and content knowledge: Validation of the COACTIV constructs. *ZDM Mathematics Education, 40,* 873–892.

Kunter, M., Blum, W., Krauss, S., Baumert, J., Klusmann, U. R., & Neubrand, M. (2013). *Cognitive activation in the mathematics classroom and professional competence of teachers.* New York: Springer.

Lasky, S. (2005). A sociocultural approach to understanding teacher identity, agency and professional vulnerability in a context of secondary school reform. *Teaching and Teacher Education, 21*, 899–916.

Leatham, K., & Peterson, B. (2010). Secondary mathematics cooperating teachers' perceptions of the purpose of student teaching. *Journal of Mathematics Teacher Education, 13*(2), 99–119.

Lee, H. S. (2005). Facilitating students' problems problem solving in a technological context: Prospective teachers' learning trajectory. *Journal of Mathematics Teacher Education, 8*, 223–254.

Lee, H., & Hollebrands, K. (2008). Preparing to teach mathematics with technology: An integrated approach to developing technological pedagogical content knowledge. *Contemporary Issues in Technology and Teacher Education, 8*, 326–341.

Lerman, S. (2000). The social turn in mathematics education research. In J. Boaler (Ed.), *Multiple perspectives on mathematics teaching and learning* (pp. 20–44). Westport, CT: Ablex.

Lerman, S. (2001). Cultural, discursive psychology: A sociocultural approach to studying the teaching and learning of mathematics. *Educational Studies in Mathematics, 46*, 87–113.

Lerman, S. (2012). Agency and identity: Mathematics teachers' stories of overcoming disadvantage. In T.-Y. Tso (Ed.), *Proceedings of the 36th Conference of the International Group for the Psychology of Mathematics Education* (Vol. 3, pp. 99–106). PME.

Levenson, E. (2013). Tasks that may occasion mathematical creativity: Teachers' choices. *Journal of Mathematics teacher education, 16*, 269–291.

Li, Y. (2012). Mathematics teacher preparation examined in an international context: Learning from the Teacher Education and Development Study in Mathematics (TEDS-M) and beyond. *ZDM Mathematics Education, 44*, 367–370.

Lin, F.-L., & Ponte, J. P. (2009). Face-to-face learning communities of prospective mathematics teachers: Studies on their professional growth. In K. Krainer & T. Wood (Eds.), *Participants in mathematics teacher education* (pp. 111–129). The Netherlands: Sense Publishers.

Lloyd, G. M. (2005). Beliefs about the teacher's role in the mathematics classroom: One student teacher's exploration in fiction and in practice. *Journal of Mathematics Teacher Education, 8*, 441–467.

Lloyd, G. M. (2006). Preservice teachers' stories of mathematics classrooms: Explorations of practice through fictional accounts. *Educational Studies in Mathematics, 63*(1), 57–87.

Magiera, M. T., van den Kieboom, L. A., & Moyer, J. C. (2013). An exploratory study of pre-service middle school teachers' knowledge of algebraic thinking. *Educational Studies in Mathematics, 84*, 93–113.

Mamolo, A., & Pali, R. (2014). Factors influencing prospective teachers' recommendations to students: Horizons, hexagons and heed. *Mathematical Thinking and Learning, 16*, 32–50.

Meagher, M., Özgün-Koca, S. A., & Edwards, M. T. (2011). Preservice teachers' experiences with advanced digital technologies: The interplay between technology in a preservice classroom and in field placements. *Contemporary Issues in Technology and Teacher Education, 11*, 243–270.

Mendick, H. (2006). *Masculinities in mathematics*. Maidenhead: Open University Press.

Mishra, P., & Koehler, M. J. (2006). Technological pedagogical content knowledge: A new framework for teacher knowledge. *Teachers College Record, 108*, 1017–1054.

Moon, K., Brenner, M. E., Jacob, B., & Okamoto, Y. (2013). Prospective secondary mathematics teachers' understanding and cognitive difficulties in making connections among representations. *Mathematical Thinking and Learning, 15*, 201–227.

Moreira, P. C., & David, M. M. (2008). Academic mathematics and mathematical knowledge needed in school teaching practice: Some conflicting elements. *Journal of Mathematics Teacher Education, 11*, 23–40.

Morris, A. K., Hiebert, J., & Spitzer, S. M. (2009). Mathematical knowledge for teaching in planning and evaluating instruction: What can preservice teachers learn? *Journal for Research in Mathematics Education, 40*, 491–529.

National Council for Accreditation of Teacher Education. (2010). *Transforming teacher education through clinical practice: A national strategy to prepare effective teachers*. Report of the Blue Ribbon Panel on Clinical Preparation and Partnerships for Improved Student Learning. Washington DC: Author.

National Council of Teachers of Mathematics. (1989). *Curriculum and evaluation standards for school mathematics*. Reston, VA: Author.

National Council of Teachers of Mathematics. (1991). *Professional standards for teaching mathematics*. Reston, VA: Author.

National Council of Teachers of Mathematics. (1995). *Assessment standards for school mathematics*. Reston, VA: Author.

National Council of Teachers of Mathematics. (2000). *Principles and standards for school mathematics*. Reston, VA: Author.

National Council of Teachers of Mathematics. (2014). *Principle to action: Ensuring mathematical success for all*. Reston, VA: Author.

National Research Council. (2010). *Preparing teachers: Building evidence for sound policy. Committee on the Study of Teacher Preparation Programs in the United States*, Center for Education. Division of Behavioral and Social Sciences and Education. Washington, DC: The National Academies Press.

Niess, M. L. (2012). Rethinking pre-service mathematics teachers' preparation: Technological, pedagogical and content knowledge (TPACK). In D. Polly, C. Mims, & K. Persichitte (Eds.), *Developing technology-rich, teacher education programs: Key issues* (pp. 316–336). IGI Global: Hershey, PA.

Nolan, K. (2012). Dispositions in the field: Viewing mathematics teacher education through the lens of Bourdieu's social field theory. *Educational Studies in Mathematics, 80*, 201–215.

Nguyen, T., Dekker, R., & Goedhart, M. (2008). Preparing Vietnamese student teachers for teaching with a student-centered approach. *Journal of Mathematics Teacher Education, 11*(1), 61–81.

Oliveira, H. (2004). Percursos de identidade do professor de Matemática em início de carreira: O contributo da formação inicial. *Quadrante, 13*(1), 115–145.

Oliveira, H., & Cyrino, M. C. (2011). A formação inicial de professores de Matemática em Portugal e no Brasil: narrativas de vulnerabilidade e agência. *Interacções, 7*, 104–113.

Pamplona, A. S., & de Carvalho, D. L. (2009). Comunidades de prática e conflitos de identidade na formação do professor de matemática que ensina estatística. In D. Fiorentini, R. C. Grando, & R. G. S. Miskulin (Eds.), *Práticas de formação e de pesquisa de professores que ensinam Matemática* (pp. 211–232). Campinas: Mercado de Letras.

Parker, D., & Adler, J. (2014). Sociological tools in the study of knowledge and practice in mathematics teacher education. *Educational Studies in Mathematics, 87*, 203–219.

Peterson, B. (2005). Student teaching in Japan: The lesson. *Journal of Mathematics Teacher Education, 8*, 61–74.

Peterson, B., & Williams, S. (2008). Learning mathematics for teaching in the student teaching experience: Two contrasting cases. *Journal of Mathematics Teacher Education, 11*, 459–478.

Ponte, J. P. (2011). Teachers' knowledge, practice, and identity: Essential aspects of teachers' learning. *Journal of Mathematics Teacher Education, 14*, 413–417.

Ponte, J. P., & Chapman, O. (2008). Preservice mathematics teachers' knowledge and development. In L. D. English (Ed.), *Handbook of international research in mathematics education: Directions for the 21st century* (2nd ed., pp. 225–263). New York: Routledge.

Ponte, J. P., & Chapman, O. (2016). Prospective mathematics teachers' learning and knowledge for teaching. In L. English & D. Kirshner (Eds.), *Handbook of international research in mathematics education* (3rd ed.). New York: Routledge.

Ponte, J. P., & Oliveira, H. (2002). Remar contra a maré: A construção do conhecimento e da identidade profissional na formação inicial. *Revista de Educação, 1*(2), 145–163.

Prediger, S. (2010). How to develop mathematics-for-teaching and for understanding: The case of meanings of the equal sign. *Journal of Mathematics Teacher Education, 13*, 73–93.

Rhine, S., Harrington, R., & Olszewski, B. (2015). The role of technology in increasing preservice teachers' anticipation of students' thinking in algebra. *Contemporary Issues in Technology and Teacher Education, 15*(2), 85–105.

Ricks, T. (2011). Process reflection during Japanese lesson study experiences by prospective secondary mathematics teachers. *Journal of Mathematics Teacher Education, 14*, 251–267.

Rhoads, K., Radu, I., & Weber, K. (2011). The teacher internship experiences of prospective high school mathematics teachers. *International Journal of Science & Mathematics Education, 9*, 999–1022.

Rhoads, K., Samkoff, A., & Weber, K. (2013). Student teacher and cooperating teacher tensions in a high school mathematics teacher internship: The case of Luis and Sheri. *Mathematics Teacher Education And Development, 15*(1), 108–128.

Ryve, A., Nilsson, P., & Mason, J. (2012). Establishing mathematics for teaching within classroom interactions in teacher education. *Educational Studies in Mathematics, 81*, 1–14.

Sachs, J. (2005). Teacher education and the development of professional identity. In P. M. Denicolo & M. Kompf (Eds.), *Connecting policy and practice: Challenges for teaching and learning in schools and universities* (pp. 5–21). New York: Routledge Farmer.

Sanchez-Matamoros, G., Fernandez, C., & Llinares, S. (2014). Developing pre-service teachers' noticing on students' understanding of the derivative concept. *International Journal of Science and Mathematics Education, 13*, 1305–1329.

Santagata, R., Zannoni, C., & Stigler, J. W. (2007). The role of lesson analysis in pre-service teacher education: An empirical investigation of teacher learning from a virtual video-based field experience. *Journal of Mathematics Teacher Education, 10*, 123–140.

Schmidt, W. H., Blömeke, S., & Tatto, M. T. (2011). *Teacher education matters: A study of middle school mathematics teacher preparation in six countries.* New York: Teacher College Press.

Shriki, A. (2010). Working like real mathematicians: Developing prospective teachers' awareness of mathematical creativity through generating new concepts. *Educational Studies in Mathematics, 73*, 159–179.

Shulman, L. S. (1986). Those who understand: Knowledge growth in teaching. *Educational Researcher, 15*, 4–14.

Sirotic, N., & Zazkis, R. (2007). Irrational numbers: The gap between formal and intuitive knowledge. *Educational Studies in Mathematics, 65*, 49–76.

Skott, J., Zoest, L. V., & Gellert, U. (2013). Theoretical frameworks in research on and with mathematics teachers. *ZDM Mathematics Education, 45*, 501–505.

Son, J. W. (2013). How preservice teachers interpret and respond to student errors: ratio and proportion in similar rectangles. *Educational Studies in Mathematics, 84*, 49–70.

Speer, N. M., King, K. D., & Howell, H. (2015). Definitions of mathematical knowledge for teaching: Using these constructs in research on secondary and college mathematics teachers. *Journal of Mathematics Teacher Education, 18*, 105–122.

Stankey, D., & Sundstrom, M. (2007). Extended analyses: Finding deep structure in standard high school mathematics. *Journal of Mathematics Teacher Education, 10*, 391–397.

Star, J. R., & Strickland, S. K. (2007). Learning to observe: Using video to improve preservice mathematics teachers' ability to notice. *Journal of Mathematics Teacher Education, 11*, 107–125.

Steele, M. D., Hillen, A. F., & Smith, M. S. (2013). Developing mathematical knowledge for teaching in a methods course: The case of function. *Journal of Mathematics Teacher Education, 16*, 451–482.

Sternberg, R. J. (1999). The nature of mathematical reasoning. In L. V. Stiff & R. Frances (Eds.), *Developing mathematical reasoning in grades K-12, 1999 Yearbook* (pp. 37–44). Reston, VA: National Council of Teachers of Mathematics.

Stylianides, G. J., Stylianides, A. J., & Philippou, G. N. (2007). Preservice teachers' knowledge of proof by mathematical induction. *Journal of Mathematics Teacher Education, 10*, 145–166.

Stockero, S. L. (2008). Using a video-Based curriculum to develop a reflective stance in prospective mathematics teachers. *Journal of Mathematics Teacher Education, 11*, 373–394.

Subramaniam, K. (2014). Prospective secondary mathematics teachers' pedagogical knowledge for teaching the estimation of length measurements. *Journal of Mathematics Teacher Education, 17*, 177–198.

Tall, D., & Vinner, S. (1981). Concept image and concept definition in mathematics with particular reference to limits ad continuity. *Educational Studies in Mathematics, 12*, 151–169.

Tatto, M. T., Lerman, S., & Novotna, J. (2010). The organization of the mathematics preparation and development of teachers: A report from the ICMI Study 15. *Journal of Mathematics Teacher Education, 13*, 313–324.

Tatto, M. T., Peck, R., Schwille, J., Bankov, K., Senk, S. L., Rodriguez, M., et al. (2012). *Policy, practice, and readiness to teach primary and secondary mathematics in 17 countries: Findings from the IEA Teacher Education and Development Study in Mathematics (TEDS-M)*. Amsterdam: International Association for the Evaluation of Educational Achievement (IEA).

Teixeira, B. R., & Cyrino, M. C. D. C. T. (2015). Desenvolvimento da Identidade Profissional de Futuros Professores de Matemática no Ambito da Orientação de Estágio. *Bolema, 29*(52), 658–680.

Ticknor, C. (2012). Situated learning in an abstract algebra classroom. *Educational Studies in Mathematics, 81*, 307–323.

Tsamir, P. (2005). Enhancing prospective teachers' knowledge of learners' intuitive conceptions: The case of same A-same B. *Journal of Mathematics Teacher Education, 8*, 469–497.

Tsamir, P. (2007). When intuition beats logic: Prospective teachers' awareness of their same sides-same angles solutions. *Educational Studies in Mathematics, 65*, 255–279.

Tsamir, P., Rasslan, S., & Dreyfus, T. (2006). Prospective teachers' reactions to right-or-wrong tasks: The case of derivatives of absolute value functions. *Journal of Mathematical Behavior, 25*, 240–251.

Van den Kieboom, L., Marta Magiera, M., & Moyer, J. (2014). Exploring the relationship between K-8 prospective teachers' algebraic thinking proficiency and the questions they pose during diagnostic algebraic thinking interviews. *Journal of Mathematics Teacher Education, 17*, 429–481.

Van Putten, S., Stols, G., & Howie, S. (2014). Do prospective mathematics teachers teach who they say they are? *Journal of Mathematics Teacher Education, 17*, 1–24.

Viseu, F., & Ponte, J. P. (2012). The tole of ICT in supporting the development of professional knowledge during teaching practice. *Mathematics Teacher Education and Development, 14*, 137–158.

Walshaw, M. (2004). Pre-service mathematics teaching in the context of schools: An exploration into the constitution of identity. *Journal of Mathematics Teacher Education, 7*, 63–86.

Walshaw, M. (2010). Mathematics pedagogical change: Rethinking identity and reflective practice. *Journal of Mathematics Teacher Education, 13*, 487–497.

Wang, T. Y., & Tang, S. J. (2013). Profiles of opportunities to learn for TEDS-M future secondary mathematics teachers. *International Journal of Mathematics and Science Education, 11*, 847–877.

Wenger, E. (1998). *Communities of practice: learning, meaning, and identity*. Cambridge University Press.

Wilson, S. M., Floden, R. E., & Ferrrini-Mundy, J. (2001). *Teacher preparation research: Current knowledge, gaps, and recommendations*. Seattle, WA: Center for the Study of Teaching and Policy.

Wilson, P. H., Lee, H. S., & Hollebrands, K. F. (2011). Understanding prospective mathematics teachers' processes for making sense of students' work with technology. *Journal for Research in Mathematics Education, 42*, 39–64.

Winsløw, C., & Durand-Guerrier, V. (2007). Education of lower secondary mathematics teachers in Denmark and France. *Nordic Studies in Mathematics Education, 12*(2), 5–32.

Yanik, H. B. (2011). Prospective middle school mathematics teachers' preconceptions of geometric translations. *Educational Studies in Mathematics, 78*, 231–260.

Yemen-Karpuzcu, S., Ulusoy, F., & Isiksal-Bostan, M. (2015). Prospective middle school mathematics teachers' covariational reasoning for interpreting dynamic events during peer interactions. *International Journal of Science and Mathematics Education* (online first). doi:10. 1007/s10763-015-9668-8.

Zazkis, D., & Zazkis, R. (2016). Prospective teachers' conceptions of proof comprehension: Revisiting a proof of the Pythagorean theorem. *International Journal of Science and Mathematics Education, 14*, 777–803.

Zbiek, R. M., & Conner, A. (2006). Beyond motivation: Exploring mathematical modeling as a context for deepening students' understandings of curricular mathematics. *Educational Studies in Mathematics, 63*, 89–112.

Zembat, I. O. (2008). Pre-service teachers' use of different types of mathematical reasoning in paper-and-pencil versus technology-supported environments. *International Journal of Mathematical Education in Science and Technology, 39* (2), 143-160.

Zengin, Y., & Tatar, E. (2015). The teaching of polar coordinates with dynamic mathematics software, *International Journal of Mathematical Education in Science and Technology, 46* (1), 127-139.

Further Readings

Further readings regarding teachers' knowledge

Ball, D.L., Blömeke, S., & Delaney, S., & Kaiser, G. (Eds.) (2012). Measuring teacher knowledge-approaches and results from a cross-national perspective. *ZDM Mathematics Education, 44*, 223-455.

Ponte, J. P., & Chapman, O. (2016). Prospective mathematics teachers' learning and knowledge for teaching. In L. English & D. Kirshner (Eds.), *Handbook of international research in mathematics education (3rd Ed.)*. New York: Routledge.

Further Readings Regarding PSMTs Preparation and Technology

Niess, M., & Gillow-Wiles, H. (2014). Transforming science and mathematics teachers' technological pedagogical content knowledge using a learning trajectory instructional approach. *Journal of Technology and Teacher Education, 22*, 497–520.

Herbst, P., Chieu, V., & Rougee, A. (2014). Approximating the practice of mathematics teaching: What learning can web-based, multimedia storyboarding software enable? *Contemporary Issues in Technology and Teacher Education, 14*(4), 356–383.

Goos, M., & Geiger, V. (2012). Connecting social perspective on mathematics teacher education in online environment. *ZDM Mathematics Education, 44*, 705–715.

Borba, M. D. C., & Llinares, S. (2012). Online mathematics teacher education: Overview of an emergent field of research. *ZDM Mathematics Education, 44*, 697–704.

Moore-Russ, D., Wilse, J., Grabowski, J., & Bampton, T. M. (2015). Perceptions of online learning spaces and their incorporation in mathematics teacher education. *Contemporary Issues in Technology and Teacher Education, 15*, 283–317.

Further Readings Regarding Teacher' Professional Identity

Black, L., Mendick, H., & Solomon, Y. (2009). *Mathematical relationships in education: Identities and participation*. New York: Routledge.

Brown, T., & McNamara, O. (2011). *Becoming a mathematics teacher: Identity and identifications*. New York: Springer.

Gellert, U., Espinoza, L., & Barbé, J. (2013). Being a mathematics teacher in times of reform. *ZDM Mathematics Education, 45*, 535–545.

Gresalfi, M. S., & Cobb, P. (2011). Negotiating identities for mathematics teaching in the context of professional development. *Journal for Research in Mathematics Education, 42*, 270–304.

Lutovac, S., & Kaasila, R. (2014). Pre-service teachers' future-oriented mathematical identity work. *Educational Studies in Mathematics, 85*, 129–142.

Further Readings Regarding PSMTs Field Experiences

Bullough, R. V, Jr., Young, J., Birrell, J. R., Clark, D. C., Egan, M. W., Erickson, L., et al. (2003). Teaching with a peer: A comparison of two models of student teaching. *Teaching and Teacher Education, 19*(1), 57–73.

Conference Board of the Mathematical Sciences. (2012). *The mathematical education of teachers II*. Providence, RI and Washington DC: American Mathematical Society and Mathematical Association of America.

Klein, E. J., Taylor, M., Onore, C., Strom, K., & Abrams, L. (2013). Finding a third space in teacher education: Creating an urban teacher residency. *Teaching Education, 24*(1), 27–57.

Leatham, K. R., & Peterson, B. E. (2010). Purposefully designing student teaching to focus on students' mathematical thinking. In J. Lott & J. Luebeck (Eds.), *Mathematics teaching: Putting research into practice at all levels (AMTE Monograph 7* (pp. 225–239). San Diego, CA: Author.